PROTECTING
YOUR RETIREMENT
from *the* FINANCIAL
PERFECT STORM

PROTECTING YOUR RETIREMENT
from the FINANCIAL PERFECT STORM

The 5 Critical Steps to a
Safe and Secure Retirement

DAN OHLWILER

Published by Advantage, Charleston, South Carolina.
Member of Advantage Media Group.

ADVANTAGE is a registered trademark and the Advantage colophon is a trademark of Advantage Media Group, Inc.

Printed in the United States of America.

ISBN: 978-1-59932-309-1
LCCN: 2012931248

This publication is designed to provide accurate and authoritative information in regard to the subject matter covered. It is sold with the understanding that the publisher is not engaged in rendering legal, accounting, or other professional services. If legal advice or other expert assistance is required, the services of a competent professional person should be sought.

Advantage Media Group is proud to be a part of the Tree Neutral® program. Tree Neutral offsets the number of trees consumed in the production and printing of this book by taking proactive steps such as planting trees in direct proportion to the number of trees used to print books. To learn more about Tree Neutral, please visit **www.treeneutral.com**. To learn more about Advantage's commitment to being a responsible steward of the environment, please visit **www.advantagefamily.com/green**

Advantage Media Group is a leading publisher of business, motivation, and self-help authors. Do you have a manuscript or book idea that you would like to have considered for publication? Please visit **www.amgbook.com** or call **1.866.775.1696**

PREFACE

After more than 30 years in the financial services industry, helping individuals and couples create safe and secure retirement plans, I have learned that people have a wide variety of issues and goals as they prepare for and experience retirement. I have presented hundreds—if not thousands—of retirement education workshops and seminars. I have sat with thousands of people who have already retired, as well as people who are preparing to retire. What I have learned over those 30 years is that retirement means something different to everyone. Each of us has a different set of hopes, dreams, goals, and desires that we would like to experience as we sail off into our retirement sunset. But in working with so many clients over the years, I have also learned that although each person's retirement is unique, there are common threads that run through each of them.

This book explains what many of these "common threads" are. I also will share with you the absolutely essential steps in setting up a safe and secure retirement plan; a retirement plan that allows you to enjoy your retirement years rather than worry whether you're going to have enough money to last you for the rest of your life; the type of retirement plan that protects your hard-earned assets from adverse risk; a plan that minimizes the money grab from Uncle Sam through ever-increasing estate and income taxes and from the devastating costs of nursing-home care; a retirement plan that will give you the peace of mind and quality of life you have earned and so richly deserve. In other words, a plan that allows you to do what I call "S.W.A.N."—Sleep Well At Night.

Working with my clients over these many years, I have seen the best and the worst our economy has to offer. I have seen the joy and comfort individuals have when they use the tried-and-true principles I discuss in this book. I have also seen the pain and anguish people experience when they don't (or won't) apply these same principles in setting up their retirement plan.

I have worked with CPAs and estate planning attorneys and assisted many of their clients with retirement planning. When I have been brought in to help in the planning process, many of these professionals refer to me as "The Retirement Professor." Not because I have a master's degree or doctorate in retirement planning, but because of the experience, expertise and proven solutions I can provide to their clients as they plan their retirement. These professionals appreciate that when their clients implement these retirement plans, they do indeed sleep well at night.

I would like to share a story with you that illustrates the S.W.A.N. concept. A farmer had a lot of work to do on his farm, so he decided to hire someone to help him with the chores. The farmer put an ad in the local newspaper for the job opening on his farm, requesting interviews with those individuals who might be interested. Many young men applied and interviewed for the position. However, one young man who interviewed for the job really intrigued the farmer. After the initial interview niceties, the farmer started to ask about the young man's qualifications. Did he have any experience with animals? Was he able to ride a horse? Could he mend fences? Just the normal questions to establish whether someone has experience with farm work. Yet the young man answered all of these questions with the same answer: *"I can sleep when the wind blows!"* The farmer was obviously perplexed, yet was also intrigued by this answer. So he hired the young man.

During the young man's first week on the job, the farmer didn't notice anything the young man did that stood out or expounded on his enigmatic answer. Then, late one night, a big windstorm hit the area. The farmer awoke and got out of bed to secure everything down. He thought the young man would also wake up and help him to make sure everything was secure. But to the farmer's dismay, the young man was still sound asleep in bed. The young man didn't get up to help at all, and the farmer was somewhat annoyed by the seemingly lazy young man.

So the farmer set about making sure everything was tied down and that all the animals were safe. When he came to the barn, he noticed that the barn door had already been secured and the cows and chickens were all inside, safe and sound. Then he went to the corral and found that all the horses were penned up and the gate had been latched and locked. He checked the windows on the house and saw that all of the storm windows were already in place. As he went around the farm, checking to see what needed to be done to withstand the windstorm, he realized that the young man had completed all of the tasks beforehand and that he had taken care of everything that needed to be done. It was then that the farmer understood what the young man meant in his interview when he said, "I can sleep when the wind blows."

When we set up our retirement plans, we want to be like that young man on the farm. We want to make sure that we can sleep well at night (S.W.A.N.) when the financial winds blow—whenever that may be.

In the following chapters, I will share with you what I have learned in 30 years of working with individuals and families to prepare, develop and implement the five safe-and-secure principles for those looking to sleep well at night in retirement. I hope you will find this information helpful as you prepare to enter retirement and sail off into the retirement sunset of your life.

CONTENTS

"THE PERFECT STORM"

A few years back, George Clooney starred in a movie called *The Perfect Storm*. Do you remember the story behind that movie? It was about fishermen, right? And normally fishing boats can withstand one storm system. But in this movie, several storm systems came together all at once and the boat was hit by these storms simultaneously. As a result, the boat ended up sinking along with all of the crew. There were no survivors. As I look at our current economic environment, I think we are in a "financial perfect storm." Why do I say that? Because there are a lot of things going on around us right now—"storms" if you will—in the financial world that can and will have an impact on our retirement. Let me mention a few of these "financial storms" that will impact us as we move forward in this discussion.

A BI-POLAR STOCK MARKET

The first financial storm is what I call a "bi-polar" stock market. What do I mean by "bi-polar"? With the stock market today, there's really no rhyme or reason to how it performs. The so-called pros say there is, but do they really know from one day to the next what the market is going to do? Absolutely not. One day the market is up 150 points, the next day it's down 250. Then down 175 points and up 125. During the market crash of 2007-2008, there were multiple times when the market dropped 500-700 points in one day. When I was growing up (yes, I know—many years ago), if the market went up or down 50 points in a single day, it was the headline news in the next day's paper. In today's market, that 50-point move would barely rate a mention on the evening news. The stock market today is not the same market it has been historically.

> *During the market crash in 2008, there were days when the market dropped 500-600 points in one day. The market today is not the same as what it's been historically.*

I believe that today's stock market is driven by two basic things. The first driver is *emotion*, which has always been a part of how the market performs. The market is, and always will be, affected by the emotions of people and how they react to news and events. Emotion is what makes the market unpredictable. Yes, you have people who claim to be able to read the trends and other vital signs of the market. They try to time when to buy and when to sell (called "timing the market"). You have contrarians who bet against the market. You have the "bulls" who always think the next big run-up is just around the corner, and sometimes they're lucky and get it right. However, it is still emotion that makes the market's performance unpredictable. No one really knows what the market is going to do. If they did, no one would ever lose money in the stock market. We'd all be millionaires because we'd all buy at the right time and sell at the right time. Yet there is *always* an element of emotion that affects how people react, and no one really knows what the market is going to do from one day to the next.

The second key element of today's stock market—one that has really transformed how the market reacts and performs—is *information*. Years ago, there were no computers or the internet to transfer information as quickly as it is today; no cell phones or instant messages; no fax machines or even next-day mail. The "pros on Wall Street" had to rely on much slower sources for their information. They couldn't trade on the floor of the stock market while on their cell phones like they can today. They didn't have the resources of the internet to get them instant information. They couldn't program their computers to trade instantly when certain events happened. They relied on the "old boy's network," which allowed them to get insider information (and which still goes on today). Yet now, at the touch of a button, we can access reams of information off the internet that wasn't available to us just a few years ago. The access to information by those on Wall Street is much quicker than it was in years past. And the stock market reacts to that information much faster as well. Computer programs that buy and trade millions of shares of stock at the touch of a button can impact the market dramatically. On May 7, 2010, the market had the biggest drop in the history of the Dow, dropping almost 1,000 points in a little over a half hour. Why and how did that happen? No one can really explain it. Eventually, the consensus by many on Wall Street was that the extreme drop came as a result of a "computer glitch" -- that is, computer programs that were automatically programmed to sell large volumes of stock when certain parameters were reached. That's easy for them to say, but it affected my retirement!

THE THREAT OF INFLATION IS VERY REAL

Another storm system in this "financial perfect storm" is the constant threat of inflation and increases in our cost of living. There's debate among many "professionals" as to whether we've actually come out of the recession of 2008. (Those professionals say we came out of the recession in June 2009.) Yet when the economy does actually come out of the recession and we see signs of a recovery, we will see inflation start to raise its ugly head.

If in fact we are experiencing very low inflation (at least according to the government), then why does everything seem to cost more!

The government tells us we don't have any inflation right now, or that if we do have inflation, it is very low. People receiving Social Security didn't get a cost-of-living adjustment in 2011 because, according to the government, "as determined by the Bureau of Labor Statistics, there is no increase in the CPI-W from the third quarter of 2008, the last year a COLA was determined, to the third quarter of 2010, therefore, under existing law, there can be no COLA in 2011."[1]

1   Social Security News release, Friday October 15, 2010

Yet if that actually is the case and there is no inflation going on, why does everything seem to cost more—at least to me? Are gas prices higher? What about the cost of food? Is the cost of health care more expensive than it was five years ago? How about the cost for a new car? It seems that in figuring out the cost-of-living adjustment for Social Security, the government conveniently omits the cost of fuel and food in their equation, and yet they use wages as one of the determining factors. And what happens to wages in a recession? The generally go down—impacting the way COLA is determined for Social Security (along with other factors).

Again, even though there is debate about whether we're still in a recession, we're still feeling the effects of the 2008 financial meltdown. Inflation haunts us every time we turn around, in one way or another. So inflation can and will have a dramatic impact on our retirement plans if we don't take it into account when we set them up.

MORE WORRIES: THE NATIONAL DEBT

Another storm system is our national debt. What's our official national debt these days--over $18 trillion dollars—and still climbing! It's projected to climb to $20 trillion by the end of President Obama's term in office. Do you know how many zeros that is? Twelve zeros ($18,000,000,000,000). That equates to over $60,000 for every man, woman, and child living in the United States. And what are some in Congress trying to do? Raise the debt level even more so they can spend more. It's unbelievable! We have to do something to address this issue or our debt will consume us. We can't continue down this path of spending.

David M. Walker, the Comptroller General of the government's General Accounting Office from 1998 to 2008, said:

> *"We suffer from a fiscal cancer. It is growing inside us. Our country would need $53 trillion invested today—which is about $175,000 per person—to deliver on the government's obligations and promises. How much of this $53 trillion do we have? Zip.…I have three grandchildren. They didn't create this problem, but it's their problem. And if policymakers don't start making tough choices soon, they're going to pay the price. It's morally wrong. And it's time we righted that wrong."*[2]

Mr. Walker said that in 2008!! What do you think those numbers would be today? So our national debt is certainly a financial storm that will affect us for years to come.

DYSFUNCTIONAL POLITICS IN AN UNSTABLE WORLD

One of the biggest problems is what I call a "dysfunctional" Congress. I'm not going to get into politics. I don't care if you are Democrat or Republican (or an Independent), but if it were up to me, I'd throw them all out and start over again. They can't seem to work with each other anymore. Democrats don't want to do anything that might make the Republicans look good, and Republicans are afraid to make

2   "I.O.U.S.A." Documentary, 2008

the Democrats look good. So neither party is able to get anything done. It seems the environment in Washington has become not so much about what is right for the county, but which party looks good. And so they have become a dysfunctional Congress, locked in this political environment of a stalemate.

The federal government's going to be bleeding money as Baby Boomers retire.

Finally, there is world politics. What do I mean by world politics? Well, what's going on all over the world? When Greece and some of the other European countries had to finally face their financial crises, what happened (and continues to happen) to our stock market? It went down! When there's a terrorist attack in another country, or there's political unrest in the Middle East, what happens to our stock market? It goes down. And countries all over the world are now recognizing that they can't continue to make promises for unfunded future benefits without it coming home to roost at some point. As a result, you are seeing protests all over the world—from the ones who were given the promises, as well as protests by the future generations who are realizing they are footing the bill. And then there's political unrest in many countries. People wanting change in their government and their leaders. And anytime there's political unrest in the world, it affects *our* stock market, which in turn affects *my* retirement! So what happens in other countries can and actually does have an impact on our retirement.

When we put all of these financial "storms" together, it creates that "financial perfect storm," which can have a devastating impact on our retirement plan—IF we don't set up safeguards against these storms. And do you know what? Many people are sitting in a lifeboat hoping to withstand the storm! You don't need to ask George Clooney to figure out how that's going to end.

THE COMING TSUNAMI OF TAXES

I believe there are going to be two "financial tsunamis" coming as a result of this perfect storm. One is a tsunami of taxes, and the other is going to be financial risk to our investments.

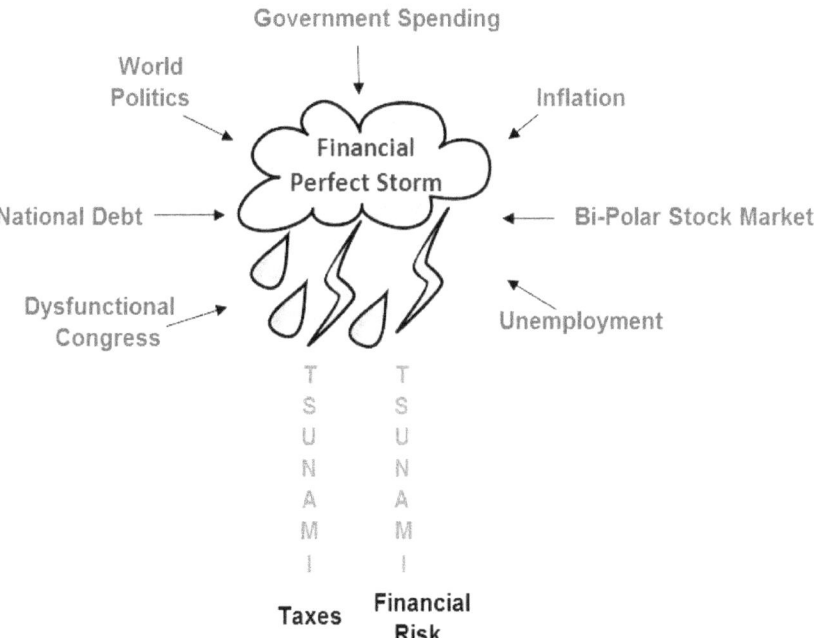

This book will show what you need to do to protect yourself and your retirement from these financial storms, and the five steps you should take in order to set up a safe and secure foundation for your retirement plan.

CHAPTER 2

STEP 1: TAX PLANNING

J ust out of curiosity, do you think taxes are going down in the future? No? Do you think *anyone* predicts taxes are going down in the future? I believe almost everyone agrees that taxes will more than likely be going up sometime in the near future. And why will they be going up? The national debt is one reason. Government spending is another. But I will tell you why taxes are probably going to go up. It's a four-letter word—M-A-T-H! The numbers just don't add up. The government has promised too much to too many people and we're spending much more than what we bring in. And it's just going to get worse.

> *"Lawmakers will look back on 2011 as the year the U.S. started down into a financial Grand Canyon, because the first Baby Boomers turn 65 this year – the front edge of a tidal wave of Baby Boomer retirements. Over the next 20 years, around 10,000 Baby Boomers will be retiring each*

day," says Andrew Biggs, an analyst at the American Enterprise Institute. That also means the members of one of the most affluent generations will slow down in buying cars and homes and consumer products of all kinds, as they pass their peak earning years and head into retirement. That could hurt the economy, but it is clearly a financial disaster for the federal government as those 79 million Boomers shift from paying taxes into Social Security and Medicare and start collecting benefits from them.

"The federal government's going to be bleeding money as the Baby Boomers retire," says Doug Holtz Eakin, a former director of the Congressional Budget Office. "We know we can't pay all the Social Security and Medicare benefits that we promised. There isn't enough money in the world to do that, so we know we're going to have to make cuts," Biggs says. "But politicians are afraid to make the choices to do that."[3]

THE BABY BOOMER TIME BOMB

The Baby Boomers are going to go from paying *into* Social Security to *receiving* Social Security. They are going to go from paying *into* Medicare to *qualifying* for Medicare. Baby Boomers are going to have a giant impact on future social spending by the government. And do you think the politicians in Washington don't know this? They absolutely do. And that's why it's so scary. The career politicians in Washington know they can't fund all of the promises that have been made to people—especially in regards to Social Security and

---

3   "Baby Boomers Could Force Economic Catastrophe." – Jim Angle, FoxNews. com

Medicare. Taxes are going to go up—they have to in order to meet the coming obligations—unless they want to default on the promises already made, which isn't a very popular road for politicians.

As comptroller general of the United States, David Walker had an inside view of what was—and is—happening to our national fiscal situation. Since as far back as 2008, he has been trying to sound a voice of alarm to anyone who will listen. Walker eventually decided to leave his job as the comptroller general in 2008 to go on a "town hall" tour across our country. Actually, he continues to raise his voice in alarm of what lies ahead, *if* we don't do something to get our fiscal house in order. He has been trying to educate and inform everyone who will listen of the real possibility of an unprecedented financial crisis we face if something isn't done—and soon. Walker recently stated:

> *I think we're going to have an adult conversation. We just need to have it sooner rather than later before we have our own U.S. debt crisis. You know, a U.S. debt crisis could come within the next two to three years. We have huge interest rate risk. We have the lowest average maturity of any sovereign nation or major nation on debt. We have historically low interest rates. We're adding debt at record rates. We have to rollover a great amount each year. Our largest holder of our debt is the Federal Reserve. I mean, that's not an arm's length transaction. Wake up Washington—we've got a problem. It's time to come to work.[4]*

---

4   Cox, Jeff. "US Finances Rank Near Worst in the World: Study." CNBC.com.

Unfortunately for all of us, to solve the crisis means we're all going to be impacted in some way as Congress looks for ways to fix the problem. For years they've just kicked the ball down the road as they promised too many things to too many people. And now the time has come to face the music. We can no longer rely on future generations to fix the problem. We—and when I say we, I mean the representatives we have elected, so there is some culpability on our part—can't continue down the path we're on. It's not possible to continue borrowing the way we have to fund those promises. Taxes *have* to go up. The numbers just don't add up if we stay on the same course.

TAXES ARE ON SALE!

Now, historically speaking, believe it or not, income taxes right now are probably at an all-time low. We might not think so every time April 15 rolls around and we are writing our income-tax checks to the IRS, but when you look at history, the top income-tax rates today are very low compared to what they have been in the past.

Marginal Tax Brackets
1932 - Present (Married filing jointly)

Year	$1,001	$20,001	$75,001	$250,001	$450,000+
1932	10%	16%	36%	56%	58%
1936	11%	19%	39%	62%	68%
1942	38%	55%	75%	85%	88%
1944	41%	59%	81%	92%	94%
1946	38%	56%	78%	89%	91%
1956	26%	38%	62%	75%	89%
1964	23%	34%	56%	66%	76%
1980	18%	24%	54%	59%	70%
2011	10%	15%	25%	35%	35%
2012-present	10%	15%	25%	33%	**39.6%**

So, if you look at history, income taxes are really "on sale" right now. They're at the lowest point they have been in decades. But why don't we feel that way? Because it seems like every time we turn around we're being hit with some kind of tax. We have income tax, sales tax, real estate taxes, personal property tax, payroll tax, gasoline tax, taxes on our plane tickets and rental cars, taxes on hotel rooms, and if that's not enough, they want taxes when we die. And it just goes on and on. On a recent vacation with my wife to Hawaii, the taxes on the rental car were actually higher than the cost of renting the car itself. It actually doubled the cost of the rental. Amazing.

Therefore, if we don't take control of our tax planning, then by default, we will get stuck with the government's tax plan. And what's the government's plan? Their plan is to take all they can get! That's

Uncle Sam's tax plan. The government actually hopes you don't do any tax planning. They hope you are part of the millions of people who just turn their tax information over to their accountant every year and wait for the "bad news" without doing any tax planning or taking advantage of the tax laws that are available to all of us. In this situation, their accountant really is just their tax preparer, not a tax advisor or planner.

TAX EVASION VERSUS TAX AVOIDANCE

There's also a difference between tax evasion and tax "avoidance." One approach is legal and the other could get you put in jail. I love the following quote by Judge Learned Hand, who served on the U.S. District Court in New York, and later served on the United States Court of Appeals in the Second District. Judge Hand said:

> *"Anyone may arrange his affairs so that his taxes shall be as low as possible; he is not bound to choose that pattern which best pays the treasury. There is not even a patriotic duty to increase one's taxes. Over and over again the courts have said that there is nothing sinister in so arranging affairs as to keep taxes as low as possible. Everyone does it, rich and poor alike, and all do right, for nobody owes any public duty to pay more than the law demands."[5]*

---

5   *Judge Learned Hand in the case of Gregory* v. Helvering 69 F.2d 809, 810 (2d Cir. 1934), aff'd, 293 U.S. 465, 55 S.Ct. 266, 79 L.Ed. 596 (1935)

CHAPTER 3

STEP #1:
TAX PLANNING
(CONTINUED)

"Tax-Infested" Accounts

"We never would have put our money into an
IRA had we known there was such a substantial
penalty for early withdrawal."

THE PENSION-LESS SOCIETY

This chapter deals with the tax-planning opportunities that people rarely utilize, but even more seriously, don't understand. As I have worked with people in retirement (or preparing to retire), I have found that in many cases the biggest asset many of them have are in what I call, "*tax-infested* accounts." These are retirement plans such as 401(k)s, IRAs, 403bs, 457 plans, any type of qualified plan where people have been able to put money in over the time they have been working and have not been taxed on it up to this point. These people have worked for 30 to 40 years and have put away large amounts of money (in addition to the contributions by employers) in these accounts, anticipating they will need the money for retirement. Many times they do need the income from these accounts to live on—and many times they don't. They might have a pension plan or other assets they are using to generate the money they need to live on a monthly basis.

The older, guaranteed pension-retirement plans that the retiring generation's parents used to have and that provided a guaranteed lifetime retirement benefit, are now becoming extinct.

For many years, companies have been moving away from assuming the risk of providing a lifetime benefit to the employee (and many times the spouse as well) in vast numbers and replacing those plans with 401(k) plans, which transfer more of the risk to the employee. The employee's retirement benefit now depends on how well the stock market performs, and the future benefit he or she receives is no longer guaranteed by the employer. We are quickly becoming a "pension-less" society.

TAXED FOREVER AND EVER

Now why do I call these "tax-infested accounts"? It is because these accounts are going to be taxed forever! The income received from these types of accounts will be taxed for the rest of your life. They will be taxed for the rest of your spouse's life (if he or she were to inherit it). And then they will still be taxed for the rest of your children's lives when they inherit these accounts (and even your grandchildren are taxed on it—if we want to take it that far). So these accounts are "forever taxed."

Accounts like IRAs, 401(k)s and other qualified retirement accounts will be taxed for the rest of the owner's life and their beneficiaries' lives as well—unless there is an exit strategy implemented.

Let's look at how these accounts work. The government allows us to deduct the contribution we make to these types of accounts off our income taxes (up to the set amount allowed), allows these funds to accumulate, and defers any taxes on the funds in those accounts. However, at some point, the IRS says, "Enough is enough. We have to start taking money out of these 'qualified' accounts." That point is when the account's owner reaches 70½ years old. It is called "Required Minimum Distributions" (RMD). These are distributions that are required to be taken out each and every year by the IRS. (By the way, do you know what I think the letters "IRS" should actually stand for? They should stand for "*I Rob Seniors!*"). Now, what happens if we don't take out the required amount? We are penalized.

Do you know how much that penalty is? *Lots*! It's 50 percent! The question is, 50 percent of what? Let's look at an example.

WHAT IS YOUR REQUIRED MINIMUM DISTRIBUTION?

Say we have a $500,000 IRA (when I use the term "IRA" throughout this book, it could just as easily be a 401(k), 403b, or any other type of qualified plan). How do you go about determining what the correct amount your required minimum distribution is?

Let's assume you are going to turn age 70½ this year and you have $500,000 in your IRA account. To figure out what your required distribution will be, you need to go to the Uniform Lifetime Distribution Table published by the IRS. Below is the table published by the Internal Revenue Service (Publication 590) for RMD calculations (this table actually goes all the way up to age 111). This table applies to all retirement accounts for individuals who have reached age 70½ and own a retirement account—IRA, 401(k), 403b, etc. (There is one exception that I will address shortly.)

Required Minimum Distribution Table

Uniform Lifetime Table

Age	Distribution Factor	Age	Distribution Factor
70	27.4	86	14.1
71	26.5	87	13.4
72	25.6	88	12.7
73	24.7	89	12.0
74	23.8	90	11.4
75	22.9	91	10.8
76	22.0	92	10.2
77	21.2	93	9.6
78	20.3	94	9.1
79	19.5	95	8.6
80	18.7	96	8.1
81	17.9	97	7.6
82	17.1	98	7.1
83	16.3	99	6.7
84	15.5	100	6.3
85	14.8	101	5.9

At age 70, the factor is 27.4. So to find your RMD for the year you turn age 70½, you would to take $500,000 and divide 27.4 into your IRA balance (as of Dec. 31 of the previous year). For this example, we are assuming your IRA balance is $500,000 on Dec. 31. That amount comes to $18,248 (for simplicity, throughout this book we will round off to the nearest dollar). That is how much you're supposed to take out for that year to meet your RMD. If we only take out $10,248, how much are we short? Approximately $8,000. The penalty then in this situation would be $4,000. So we would pay a 50 percent penalty on any amount we *should* have taken—but didn't. Plus, then we still have to go back and take out the $8,000 we should have taken in the first place, which creates additional taxable income as well. So you don't want to miss taking out your required minimum distributions.

If you don't take your RMD, does Uncle Sam come knocking on your door? Not necessarily. Does the IRS knock on your door if you don't pay your income taxes? Sometimes they do, sometimes they don't. When do you get hit with the penalty if you don't take out an RMD? When they find out and then come knocking on your door or send you a letter asking about it.

If the owner of a qualified plan forgets (or doesn't take) the right required minimum distribution, the penalty is 50 percent.

Now, when you turn age 70½, what is the deadline for you to take out your first distribution? It must be taken out by April 1 of the year following the date you turn 70½. So if you turn 70½ in June, you have to take your first distribution by April 1 of the following year. But if you do wait until April of the next year, you will have two distributions in that year; one distribution for the previous year in which you turned 70½ and one distribution for the current year when you are age 71. Therefore, you may want to do some tax planning and take out your first RMD before Dec. 31 in the year that you turn 70½, to eliminate a double distribution the following year. Again, it will depend on your tax bracket and your income planning as to when you would (or should) take your first RMD from those accounts.

MULTIPLE RETIREMENT ACCOUNTS

Now, if you have an IRA with a bank, and an IRA with a mutual fund, and an IRA with an insurance company, and another one with a brokerage house, you must add up the value of all those accounts and then determine what your RMD distribution is using the Required Minimum Distribution Table. As stated earlier, the value of those accounts are determined as of Dec. 31 of the previous year. Once you determine what your RMD is, can you then take your total RMD from just one of your IRAs or 401(k)? Yes, you can. You are not required to take RMDs from each account, as long as you take the required total amount, even if it's from just one account. However, you do want to make sure you take the total amount required for that particular year.

Is there ever a time when we don't have to take out a Required Minimum Distribution once we reach age 70½? In 2009, Congress said that because of the stock market crash, we didn't have to take out a distribution that year.[6] Another exception—you don't have to take an RMD out of one of these accounts if you're still working for the company where your qualified account is, and you're still contributing to that account (e.g., 401(k)). If you have other, separate IRAs or retirement accounts that are not associated with your current employer, you still must take out your RMDs from those accounts once you turn that magic age of 70½. Finally, there are also no RMDs required from a Roth IRA.

ROTH IRA VERSUS TRADITIONAL IRA

Roth IRA retirement accounts are named after Sen. William Roth of Delaware, who was able to get legislation passed in 1997 that established tax-free IRA accounts. This is why they are now known as a Roth IRAs.[6]

What is the advantage of a Roth IRA (and now there are Roth 401(k)s as well) versus a traditional IRA account? First, all income and distributions from Roth accounts are tax-free, not only to the owner of the Roth IRA, but also to their beneficiaries (and all future beneficiaries if the Roth is still around by then). If that's the case, then why don't we all contribute or transfer all of our retirement accounts to a Roth IRA? The most common reason many of us don't use Roth accounts is because we're all usually concerned about our taxes *today*, rather than what impact taxes will have on us in the future. We'd rather get a tax deduction now and worry about our taxes later. That's what CPAs tell us, right? Get deductions today and we'll worry about the taxes later. So most of us would rather defer and delay paying taxes as long as we can—whether or not it's the right tax-planning strategy in the long run. CPAs are hard-wired to reduce taxes today rather than really looking at long-term tax planning. If they can reduce a client's current tax burden, then they will look good and the client is usually happy.

WHAT IS YOUR EXIT STRATEGY?

The problem is that most times CPAs and employees never plan an "exit strategy" for these accounts. They just worry about deferring taxes as long as possible, thinking that taxes will be lower when they

---

6   Taxpayer Relief Act of 1997

retire. Yet, as we discussed earlier, we all feel like taxes will more than likely being going *up* in the future—not down.

Many CPAs are hard-wired to reduce taxes in the short term rather than really looking at long-term tax planning.

BUY NOW, PAY LATER

There's another thing people don't realize when contributing to a traditional IRA or other retirement accounts. Uncle Sam has learned that he is more than willing to give you a current tax deduction for a $5,500 IRA contribution ($6,500 for those over age 50), and let it accumulate for 20-to-30 years, but then the IRS will be more than happy to collect taxes on maybe $30,000-$35,000 (depending on investment returns). So you get a tax deduction of $5,500, which if you're in a 35 percent tax bracket, saves you $1,925 in taxes. Yet, when you retire and pay taxes on that IRA, you could end up paying anywhere from 10-20 times more than the $1,925 you saved in taxes.

I want to relate a funny analogy that many of us men have experienced with our wives. I want to ask you men this question: Has your wife ever come home from shopping and said to you, "Honey, you're not going to believe how much money I saved you today"? How do we translate that sentence? It usually means they've spent money or bought something. But they bought it on *sale*, right?

Let me ask you another question. Historically speaking, are taxes "on sale" right now? We discussed earlier how our federal income-tax brackets today are at their lowest-ever rates in many cases, and we all agreed that tax rates will more than likely go up in the future. So in reality, taxes are hypothetically on sale right now. So why don't we all convert our traditional IRAs to a Roth now before income-tax rates go up? Why don't we take advantage of these low rates right now and do some tax planning for the future?

IS A ROTH IRA RIGHT FOR YOU?

Converting to a Roth IRA may not always make sense—it depends on the needs of each individual.

The truth is that conversion to a Roth IRA might or might not be a good option, depending on each individual's situation. When I talk with people about possible tax-planning opportunities and exit strategies for their retirement accounts, the first thing they always want to know is whether they should convert to a Roth IRA. Before I answer this question, I always ask them a few questions to find out what this money is going to be used for. Do you need the assets or income from your IRA in order to meet your living needs? Is this account just going to be left to your kids when you die? If they do need the income or assets to live on to meet their needs, then generally speaking, they probably shouldn't convert to a Roth IRA, because they would end up losing too much money in taxes being sent to Washington.

Let's use our example again. We have our $500,000 in a traditional IRA or 401(k) and we want to convert those funds to a Roth IRA. Can we do that? Absolutely we can. (There are earned income limitations in regards to *contributing* to a Roth account; however, there are no limitations on *converting* existing IRA/401(k) accounts to Roth.) But what's going to happen if we convert those funds to a Roth account? We have to claim the entire $500,000 as ordinary income in the year we convert, and as a result, we have to pay taxes on the entire $500,000. Obviously, if we add $500,000 to our taxable income, it would more than likely put us into the highest federal tax bracket, and we still might have state taxes that come into play as well. In California, where I live, that $500,000 would probably put you into a combined tax bracket of a minimum 40 percent (based on current tax rates). If that's the case, we would end up losing $200,000 in taxes when we covert our $500,000 to a Roth account. That would leave us with $300,000 in our Roth IRA. While that amount would now be tax-free, it will be a much smaller amount to provide income to us the rest of our lives. So, converting to a Roth account is not always the best approach as an exit strategy—IF we are going to need the income or use of the assets to meet our living expenses.

So when would be a good time to consider converting to Roth IRA?

EXIT STRATEGIES

There are a number of different exit strategies we can utilize to reduce the taxes we (and our heirs) ultimately will end up paying on these types of accounts. And which strategy to use will depend on what the ultimate goal is. Is your goal keeping control of the money to make sure you don't run out? Maximizing the money left to your children?

Paying the least amount in income and/or estate taxes? People have a variety of different goals (or a combination of several goals), and the key to successful tax planning is developing an exit strategy to match those intended goals.

If someone doesn't need the income from their IRA account and their prime goal is to pass these funds onto their children (or grandchildren), then there are several opportunities to do some long-term tax planning for these "tax-infested" accounts. The key is to take action now while tax rates are low (at least lower than what they're going to be in the future). The challenge is getting people to understand the long-term outlook of taxes and the impact they have on these accounts, and how much they will end up paying in taxes, not only over their lifetime, but their heirs' lifetimes as well.

> *Unless there's some type of exit strategy and tax planning for these accounts, people could end up paying maybe two or three times more the amount in taxes than they need to.*

Let's use our example again—our $500,000 IRA. If you don't need the income (or assets) that comes as a result of your RMD, what do you do with the required minimum distribution you are required to take each year? Most of the time when I ask people this question, they say they just spend it, or they put it in the bank or somewhere else where it isn't making much money (or they give it to their children or grandchildren). If that's the case, then there are some great opportunities to do some very effective tax planning and exit strategies for traditional IRA accounts.

EXIT STRATEGIES FOR TRADITIONAL IRAS

If the money in this IRA is ultimately going to be left to your children, how long are your children going to be taxed on it when they inherit it? Again, for the rest of their lives! And how long are *their* children (your grandchildren) going to be taxed on it if they inherit it? For the rest of their lives as well.

Now, let's assume at the age of 70, Dad has an IRA and he then takes distributions for the next 20 years. Every year, he figures out what his RMD is (or someone figures it out for him) and he takes out that distribution. He ends up paying $173,604 in taxes over the next 20 years in RMD (based on a conservative 5 percent return over the 20 years and a 30 percent tax rate).

Dad passes away and leaves Mom, who is now 88 years old, his IRA money. His IRA has been earning money over those 20 years—let's assume the 5 percent again, so that Dad's IRA is worth approximately $431,000 when Mom inherits it. Mom has two options: she can cash in the IRA and pay taxes on the lump sum, or she can take required distributions based on her age. If she doesn't want to pay taxes on the lump sum, how long is she going to be taxed on this account? That's right, for the rest of her life. Mom now lives for another five years and ends up having to take another $175,699 in RMD distributions, on which she pays $52,701 in taxes as well.

Then when Mom passes away, the IRA is inherited by the children. What are their options? Same as Mom's! They can either cash in the IRA and pay taxes on the lump-sum distribution, or they have the option of doing a "stretch IRA." (A "stretch IRA" was established in 2001 when Congress passed legislation[7] allowing the heirs of IRA owners to take RMDs from inherited IRAs rather than having to take lump-sum distributions and pay taxes on the entire amount.) And how long are the children going to be taxed on that IRA if they decide to stretch this inherited IRA? The rest of their lives (maybe another 20-25 years, or more). Prior to that "stretch IRA" legislation, beneficiaries had to have inherited retirement accounts distributed within five years of death, and pay the taxes on those distributions.

So Mom has now passed away. Let's say she has a son or daughter who is 55. They can either cash in the IRA and pay taxes on it, or they can stretch out the RMDs based upon their own life expectancy. Yet their RMD calculation is based on the "Single Life Expectancy Table for Inherited IRAs." (It's not the Uniform Lifetime Table used by Mom and Dad—it is a single life table for inherited retirement accounts.) This table actually goes up to age 111; however, for this discussion we are just showing to age 74).

---

7   The Economic Growth and Tax Relief Act Reconciliation Act of 2001

SINGLE LIFE EXPECTANCY TABLE FOR INHERITED IRAS									
	Life		Life		Life		Life		Life
Age of IRA	Expectancy	Age of IRA	Expectancy	Age of IRA	Expectancy	Age of IRA	Expectancy	Age of IRA	Expectancy
Beneficiary	(in years)	Beneficiary	(in years)	Beneficiary	(in years)	Beneficiary	(in years)	Beneficiary	(in years)
0	82.4	15	67.9	30	53.3	45	38.8	60	25.2
1	81.6	16	66.9	31	52.4	46	37.9	61	24.4
2	80.6	17	66.0	32	51.4	47	37.0	62	23.5
3	79.7	18	65.0	33	50.4	48	36.0	63	22.7
4	78.7	19	64.0	34	49.4	49	35.1	64	21.8
5	77.7	20	63.0	35	48.5	50	34.2	65	21.0
6	76.7	21	62.1	36	47.5	51	33.3	66	20.2
7	75.8	22	61.1	37	46.5	52	32.3	67	19.4
8	74.8	23	60.1	38	45.6	53	31.4	68	18.6
9	73.8	24	59.1	39	44.6	54	30.5	69	17.8
10	72.8	25	58.2	40	43.6	55	29.6	70	17.0
11	71.8	26	57.2	41	42.7	56	28.7	71	16.3
12	70.8	27	56.2	42	41.7	57	27.9	72	15.5
13	69.9	28	55.3	43	40.7	58	27.0	73	14.8
14	68.9	29	54.3	44	39.8	59	26.1	74	14.1

So for this son or daughter, who is age 55 when Mom passed away, the RMD factor for their age is 29.6. Let's assume the balance of the IRA when they inherited is now $400,000. Their required distribution would be $13,513, and they have until April 1 of the year following the death of Mom to take their first distribution. If they don't, then the 50 percent penalty applies. I had a CPA refer a client to me because he knew our firm dealt a lot with distribution planning for IRAs. The client was a 28-year-old man who had inherited his father's IRA four years prior when his father died. I asked him, *"Have you been taking out your required minimum distributions?"* You know what he said to me? He said, *"What's that?"* He didn't even know what a required distribution was! (Most children don't.) He had four years of penalties at 50 percent because he hadn't been taking out his RMDs.

Let's look at another issue—I call it a problem—that isn't usually addressed in the planning process. Is this IRA still earning money? We hope that it is (rather than losing money!). What do you think would be a conservative return over a 15-20 year period? We've used 5 percent in our previous examples. Would 5 percent be a fair number to use over the next 15-20 years? If so, then how much will this $400,000 inherited IRA earn in a year at a 5 percent? The answer is $20,000. And how much did the 55-year-old son or daughter have to take out in required distributions in the first year? Let's say $13,500 to round it off. So you have approximately $6,500 left over. What happens to the IRA then? It starts to grow larger.

When these accounts are inherited, the IRA is getting bigger and bigger over time, because the required distributions are hopefully smaller than the interest being earned by these accounts. So do you know what is happening? You're actually passing on a larger tax burden to your kids. People don't realize that they actually have a "twin brother" with their retirement accounts, and that twin brother is Uncle Sam. The bigger your retirement account gets, the bigger your twin brother gets. So unless we design some type of exit strategy for these accounts, and get the money out of these "forever taxed" accounts, Uncle Sam will continue to receive taxes forever.

I have had many people tell me, "Dan, I don't care about the taxes once I'm gone. That's my kids' problem. They can do what they want." My question to them is: Why work all your life and save all this money and then give the government more (in taxes) than you need to? Using our example of $400,000 being inherited by the son, do you know how much Mom and Dad AND their son end up paying in taxes over their lifetimes? They could end up paying *more than* $500,000 in taxes (depending on how long the son lives and the investment return on the IRA). So if one of your goals is to reduce the amount of taxes paid on this money, then leaving the money in a traditional IRA may not be the best strategy.

Why work all of your life and save all this money, and then give more than you need to in taxes to Uncle Sam?

I'm not saying we should all run out and convert to Roth IRAs because, as I explained, the decision really depends on what you want this money to do for you and what your long-term goals are. What I am saying is that if people don't have any type of exit strategies for these accounts, sticking their heads in the sand and hoping the problem goes away isn't going to work. All we've done is pass a tax burden onto our beneficiary. In fact, more than likely, the problem will get worse. We discussed earlier that income taxes are more likely to go up than down in the future. What we've done is compounded the problem for our heirs because they will probably be paying taxes on their required distributions at a higher tax rate.

So what are some options you can do now to go about setting up an exit strategy for these types of accounts? Let me share with you just one idea that I have used with clients who don't need the income from their required distributions and can utilize that income for some type of tax planning.

FROM FOREVER TAXED
TO NEVER TAXED

We have our $500,000 in an IRA. How much do we have to take out starting the first year at age 70½? We showed using the Uniform Lifetime Table that our first required distribution is $18,248. Let's assume we are in a 30 percent tax bracket. Our after-tax return on this distribution is $12,774. Generally, if we don't need that income, what do we do after we take this out? Spend it, put it in a bank at very low rates, or give it to the grandkids. Many times people ask me if they can contribute their required distributions into a Roth IRA. Sorry, the tax code does not allow required distributions to be put into a Roth IRA or other retirement account.[8]

What if we took this $12,744 and used the distribution to purchase a $500,000 life insurance policy on Dad (who is the owner of the IRA)? Every year Dad takes out his required distribution, we use the after-tax money to pay the premium on this life insurance policy. Dad then passes away and he leaves his IRA to Mom. Can Mom now convert this traditional IRA to Roth IRA? Absolutely. However, *non-spouse* beneficiaries cannot convert a traditional IRA to a Roth once the owner passes away.[9] That's why it's so important to set your exit strategy in place prior to the death of the owner of the IRA.

---

8   IRS Publication 590, Chapter 1, page 29
9   IRS Publication 590, Chapter 1, page 27

So if Mom does convert this traditional IRA to a Roth, what happens? Taxes are due on the amount she converts. How much in taxes? That depends on her tax bracket, but we'll assume because of the conversion, her income tax bracket would probably be the highest. For this discussion, that means her income tax on the conversion would be 40 percent. That would create a tax bill of $200,000, leaving Mom with a net after-tax amount of $300,000.

Yet Mom will also receive a *tax-free* death benefit of $500,000 from Dad's life insurance policy, and she could then turn around and pay the $200,000 tax bill to Uncle Sam and leave the entire $500,000 in the Roth IRA, which would then be tax-free income for the rest of her life, the rest of her children's lives, and her grandchildren's lives (if it got that far). So this account would go from a "forever taxed" to a "never taxed" account. And Mom would still have an additional $300,000 left over from the life insurance proceeds.

> *We can go from a "forever taxed" account to a "never taxed" account—if we act now and implement an exit strategy.*

This is just one strategy (among many) that we can use to design an exit strategy for these "tax-infested" accounts. The key is to determine your ultimate goal and then design your strategy around that goal. It can be done, but it requires that you take action now, rather than after the owner of the IRA passes away. The real issue usually isn't with an IRA going from one spouse to another. The planning issues usually arise when these accounts are inherited by the kids (or other heirs). That's where the problems start, and in the next chapter, I'm going to talk about the problems that can occur when children inherit IRAs.

CHAPTER 4

STEP #1: TAX PLANNING (CONTINUED)

Beneficiary Planning for Retirement Accounts

"That's me – before taxes"

Let's review what we have talked about so far. When you leave your retirement accounts to your children, they have two opportunities available to them: 1.) They can cash in the IRA and pay the taxes on the lump sum; or 2.) They can utilize the "stretch" IRA and take the required distributions based on their age at the time they inherit it. Obviously what the children do will probably depend on each individual child.

So if you leave a $500,000 IRA to a 25-year-old son or daughter, do you think they will only take out their required distribution of approximately $7,000 (for their first distribution) and leave the rest in the IRA? When I give public seminars and ask the audience this question, they all laugh and say, "Absolutely not!" The reason the audience laughs is because they know their children and their spending habits.

SAVING YOUR CHILDREN FROM THEMSELVES

I have worked with retirees over the past 30-plus years, and I have done an "unscientific" study. No surveys, just observation. I have come to the conclusion that if a couple has three or more children (they have to have at least three for this observation to be valid), most of the time—not always, but most of the time, one of those kids is a financial idiot! Not in the sense that they are mentally incompetent, but in the fact that they don't know how to handle money. They spend it on things which many times are "wants" rather than "needs." They accumulate debt recklessly without any concern for the future. They can't seem to keep a penny in their pocket. Plain and simple, this kid just doesn't know how to handle money. More likely than not, each family has one of these financial idiots!

So what is a 25-year-old going to do with the money in this IRA? More than likely they're going to spend it! On what? New cars, boats, home remodeling—the list goes on and on. If you research this on the internet, you'll find surveys that say the average inheritance in the United States is spent anywhere from 14-18 months after heirs inherit it. And do you know who benefits the most from inheritances? New car dealerships! The 25-year-old runs out and buys the new red Porsche he's dreamed about since high school. So he cashes in the $500,000 IRA. He pays probably $200,000 in taxes and is now driving his dream car, but the IRA is almost gone. This isn't always the case, but many times it is true to form (except instead of a Porsche, it might be a BMW, Mercedes, or Corvette).

So if Dad has an IRA, and let's say he has three children. One of his children is 43 years old, married with two kids. His second child is 38 years old and married. And his last child is a 28-year-old idiot!

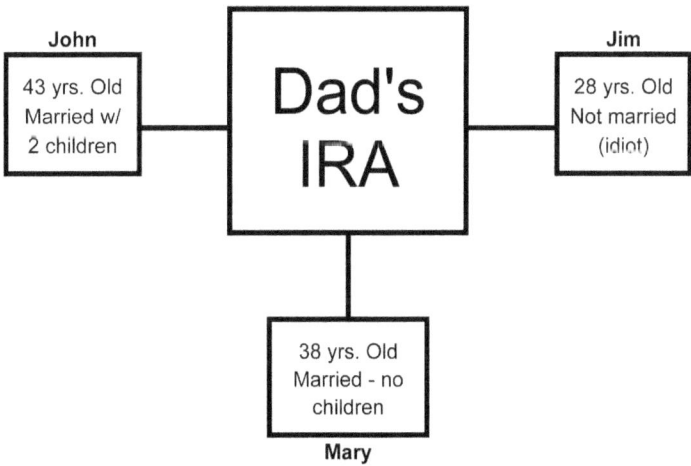

Let me ask you this: Do you think the hopes and dreams of John, the 43-year-old, are different than Jim, the 28-year-old? Probably so. John is married with two kids; he probably has a house, a mortgage to pay, and kids to put through college. He probably has a much better understanding of what life is really about. If you were his father, you could leave this $500,000 to John and he'd most likely use it wisely. He'd probably stretch it out for the time being and then figure out a long-term program for the money.

What is Jim, the 28-year-old, worried about? Many times he's not worried about much, right? If you left the $500,000 to Jim, what would happen? The money would probably be gone in a very short period of time. Do you think Jim would be worried about finding a job if he was left $500,000? Probably not. He would probably think life is great and have a great time until the money runs out. Yet if you structured the IRA in a way so that the payout to Jim was paid in a monthly (or quarterly) income stream, then you've probably done him a favor. You've helped him learn about budgeting as well as prevented him from cashing it in and giving Uncle Sam a huge tax payment.

The average inheritance in the United States is spent within 2½ years!

DESIGNATED BENEFICIARY FORMS

Now when you pass away, you need to ask yourself, will your IRA (or other retirement accounts) go where (and to whom) you want it to go to? And will the funds be distributed the way you want them to be? Retirement accounts are all distributed by how you set up your designated beneficiary form. So you need to make sure the wording on your beneficiary form is put down in such a way that those whom you want to receive this money are the ones who actually do receive it.

If we name our children as primary beneficiaries, we have to keep in mind that unfortunately, things do happen in life. Sometimes things happen to children, either through accident, health issues, divorce, or a variety of things. Let's suppose one of the three children in our example passes away before Dad does. So, if Dad has designated John, Mary, and Jim as primary beneficiaries on his beneficiary form on his IRA, and then somebody runs a red light. All of a sudden John, the 43-year-old, is standing at the Pearly Gates. And in his grief, Dad forgets to change the beneficiary form on his IRA, and then a few years later, Dad dies. His beneficiary form still has John, Mary, and Jim as the primary beneficiaries; however, John has already passed away. What happens to John's share? Does John's portion go to John's wife? John's two children? The remaining beneficiaries Mary and Jim?

> *Courts have ruled that designated beneficiary forms for retirement accounts can even supersede estate and divorce documents.*

You know where it goes? It more than likely goes to probate. Because who does Dad's beneficiary form still say the IRA goes to? Dad's IRA beneficiary form says it goes to *John*, Mary, and Jim. And because John isn't around (he's passed away), the courts have to decide who gets John's share. The courts get to decide whether it goes to John's wife, his kids, or to Mary and Jim. So you want to make sure that your beneficiary statements are up to date and current, so the money goes where and to whom you want it to.

If Dad wants to make sure John's share goes to John's children (his grandchildren) in the event John isn't alive, then he can use an option called *"Per Stirpes."* This is a Latin term used in estate distribution which basically says that if a beneficiary of an estate is not living at the time the estate is distributed, then the money the deceased person would have received goes directly to his offspring (his children—not his wife). So Dad's beneficiary form could say that he leaves his IRA to John, Mary and Jim—split equally, *per stirpes.* Then if John (or any of the three children) passes away before Dad does, and Dad forgets to change his beneficiary form, John's two children would receive John's portion of the IRA—not his wife, nor his brother and sister (Mary and Jim).

If one of the children passes away before Dad does without Dad changing the beneficiary form, and Dad would rather have his two remaining children (Mary and Jim) get the money, then his beneficiary form could say: John, Mary and Jim, split equally *if surviving.* If not, then split equally among surviving beneficiaries. The key is to make sure you keep your beneficiary forms up to date and current. Make sure your money will go where you want it to and to whom you want.

CAUTIONARY TALE: WHAT HAPPENS WHEN YOU DON'T PREPARE CORRECTLY

Let me give you a personal example I dealt with some years ago.

I had a couple come in to talk about doing some tax planning for their IRA, and stretch IRAs had just started to become popular. They had come to one of my public workshops and wanted to speak with me because the woman had a large IRA account, and they were worried about the taxes they and their heirs would have to pay on it. They brought their son in with them, which was fine. I encourage clients to bring in their children if they want to. (Sometimes they want their children there, but most of the time they don't.) So we started talking about the concept of a stretch IRA—stretching it out so it wouldn't be taxed all at once when the children inherited it, proper beneficiary statements, etc. During the course of our discussion, the son said to me, "Dan, don't worry about the beneficiary forms and the stretch IRA, I've already looked into the stretch IRA, done some reading on it and I know how to take care of it and will fill out the beneficiary forms." I said, "OK, great." And I made a note in their file that the son was going to make sure everything was in order.

Well, I got a call about three or four years later from the son and he said, "My mom has had a stroke, she's in the hospital, I'm not sure if she's going to make it." I asked him, "Do you have all your beneficiary forms in order?" He said "Yes, I have everything in order." About three days later, he called back and said, "My dad's had a heart attack, he's in the hospital, I'm not sure he's going to make it." I then asked him, "Do you have your powers of attorney in place?" He indicated that they did. I said, "OK, great."

About two to three weeks passed and I got another call from the son and he said, "About three days after I last talked to you, my mom didn't make it and passed away. Two days after that, when my dad found out that my mom passed away, he had another heart attack and passed away. Both of my parents are dead. Can I come talk to you?" I said, "Sure." When he came in for the appointment, I learned that he had set up his mother's beneficiary form in the following format:

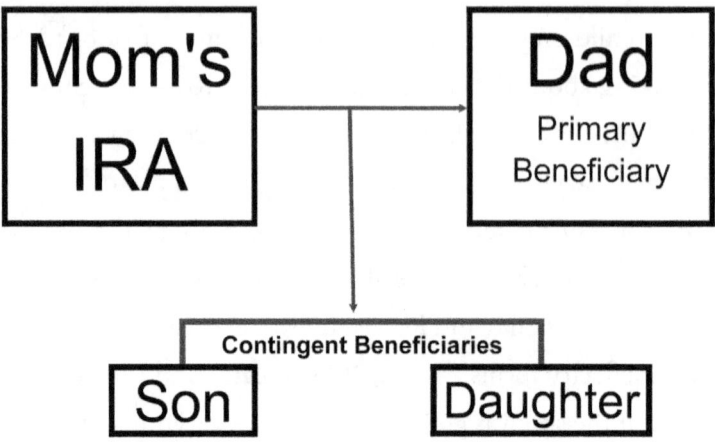

The son had set up his mother's IRA and made his father the primary beneficiary. However, if his father wasn't alive, the IRA would go to the two children as contingent beneficiaries. Is that a common scenario? Happens all the time. So let's look at this for a minute.

> *Distribution planning is one of the most complicated areas that we have in our tax code. If it isn't done correctly, it can create nightmares for your heirs.*

When Mom passed away, who became the owner of the IRA? Dad did, because he was still living at the time of Mom's death. If Dad had died within 24 hours of Mom, then the contingent beneficiaries would become the owners of the IRA. But because he lived for more than 24 hours, Dad became the legal owner. And because Dad hadn't named any beneficiaries on what was now his IRA account, what happened? It went to probate to determine who got the money.

It took approximately nine months in the probate system to get the money distributed to the children, and eventually cost them about $50,000 in attorney fees and taxes—because their son was going to "take care of it" and make sure it was done correctly.

I want to emphasize how things can get complicated if the beneficiary forms are not filled out correctly from qualified plans. CPAs and even some estate planning attorneys understand how to file income taxes and formulate estate plans, but many (if not most) of them they don't understand the distribution laws for these types of plans.

CAUTIONARY TALE: DOUBLE-CHECK YOUR BENEFICIARIES

There was an article in the *New York Post* some years ago called "*Pension Pickle.*"[10] It was the story of a guy by the name of Bruce Freidman and his wife, Anne. Bruce had been married to Anne for about 20 years. Anne was working as a teacher and was part of the teacher's pension system of New York for about 27 years. (She started teaching seven years prior to meeting her husband.)

Every year Anne received her annual statement from the pension plan and it indicated that no beneficiary had been named on her pension plan. However, it also stated that in the event that no beneficiary had been named, any remaining benefits would go to the nearest relative. And who was the nearest relative of Anne? Her husband, Bruce. So they figured everything was OK because if something ever happened to Bruce first, then the pension would go to any of her

---

10 *New York Post,* January 31, 2005

other extended relatives. However, if Anne died before Bruce, then they assumed Bruce would be considered the nearest relative and he would end up with the money.

Well, Anne had an unexpected sudden heart attack and died. After Bruce filed the claim with the pension plan, during the process of review, the pension plan found a beneficiary form that had been filled out *27* years before, when she had first started working as a teacher, and four years before Anne and Bruce had met on a blind date. At that time, Anne had named her mother, her uncle and her sister as beneficiaries. Her mother and uncle had since passed away. Who do you think got the money? The sister did, and she wouldn't talk to Bruce. More than $900,000 was in Anne's retirement account. Here is what the article said:

> *"A Manhattan Supreme Court ruling held that Anne's intention of making her husband the beneficiary could not be assumed and that the paperwork on file was clear, said Joseph Harbeson of the Corporation Counsel's office, which is representing the retirement system.*
>
> *'We feel we're complying with the law as it stands.'*
> *The Supreme Court decision was upheld by the Appellate Division in December.*
>
> *….Friedman's lawyer, Sanford Young, described last month's decision as 'sobering,' and added some advice for all couples:*

'Make sure you update your pension beneficiary forms. If you don't, your spouse and family may wind up with nothing.'"[11]

Here is one final example on making sure you review and keep your beneficiary statements current. This case is really scary. It involves a case between a daughter and her mother and it made its way all the way to the United States Supreme Court.[12]

A man and his wife had been married for 35 years. As sometimes happens in life, they decided that they didn't love each other anymore and they wanted to get a divorce. Many times, one of the biggest assets in divorce negotiations (especially one in which the man has worked in corporate America for many years) is the man's retirement account or accounts. In this situation, it was his 401(k) plan consisting of hundreds of thousands of dollars. The attorneys negotiated back and forth, and finally the wife decided that she would waive all rights to the retirement account in exchange for other assets (such as the house, or stock or other assets). So in the divorce decree, the wife waived all rights to the assets in the man's 401(k) plan. She signed a document forfeiting any claim on the retirement account in exchange for other assets. The document was notarized and finalized by the court and everyone was in agreement. The ex-husband then wanted the money in his retirement account to go to his daughter and he thought everything was OK because the wife had waived all rights to it.

Life went on and the man never changed the beneficiary form for his 401(k) listing his daughter as primary beneficiary. He assumed it was OK because he had the signed divorce agreement with the wife,

---

11   *New York Post*, January 31, 2005
12   Kennedy vs. Plan Administrator for DuPont Savings and Investment Plan et al, January 9, 2009

waiving all rights to the IRA, and his daughter was already listed as the "contingent" beneficiary. However, his ex-wife was still listed on the account as the primary beneficiary.

The man had a heart attack and died. Who does the beneficiary form still say is the primary beneficiary? The ex-wife. Who do you think the 401(k) administrator paid the money to? The ex-wife! So what did the daughter end up having to do? She sued her mother in court for the money in the 401(k). Do you think this is what her father wanted? Not even close. So the daughter sued her mother and the mother won a round in court, then the daughter appealed and she won a round. Then the mother appealed and won a round. The case made its way all the way to the U.S. Supreme Court and you know how the Supreme Court ruled? The court basically said, "We don't know for sure what the man had on his mind the day that he died." So the beneficiary statement outweighed the divorce decree. The ex-wife got the money.

I cite these examples because these are real-life stories. They can happen to real live people like us—*if* we don't do proper tax and distribution planning for our retirement accounts. Most of the time our children aren't aware of these things or they don't know what their options are when they inherit a retirement account. For example, do your children know they even have to take required distributions from an inherited IRA, no matter what their age is? Do they know *by which date* they have to take their first required distribution? If the kids take the inherited IRA and roll it into their own 401(k) or IRA, what happens? They cannot roll an inherited IRA or 401(k) into their own plan. It has to remain as an inherited IRA and properly titled as such. And if they don't title the inherited IRAs correctly, then it can also create an immediate taxable event on the entire balance they inherit. These are all things I find most heirs don't even know they have to do to handle inherited retirement accounts.

Beneficiaries usually don't understand what needs to be done with qualified retirement accounts when they inherit them in order to avoid a large tax bill.

I've had many people ask me if they can just make their living trust the beneficiary of their IRA, that way they can have the trust distribute the money the way they want. The answer is yes, you can list a living trust as your beneficiary on your retirement account. However, if you do this, you take some tax and distribution planning opportunities away from your heirs and limit the options available to them. You can set up what I call an "IRA Distribution Trust," which is a stand-alone trust, separate from your living trust, which is created strictly for retirement accounts. The only assets that would be funding this trust are retirement accounts and the only beneficiaries would be living individuals (no non-living beneficiaries like charities). This type of planning is generally only worthwhile for fairly large retirement accounts. As always, the planning process just depends on each situation and what your ultimate goal is.

A GENERATION OF SPENDERS

Let me conclude this section with a story, to emphasize the point of what happens when we leave lump sums of money to our younger children. It's a story that happened a few years ago with my family over Thanksgiving.

My wife and I have five children. (Yes, five!) All are grown and out of the house, and we decided we wanted to bring everyone home for Thanksgiving. So we made arrangements for all of them to come back into town and looked forward to an enjoyable weekend.

My wife spent a considerable amount of time, effort and preparation getting everything ready and she wanted it to be a great get-together. She spent days prior to Thanksgiving cleaning the house and getting all of the food ready, much like many women do when there's a big get-together at their homes. Well, what do men usually do on Thanksgiving (other than eat)? We watch football! That's no different in our family. We have four boys and that's one of the things we do on Thanksgiving. We watch football.

All of the kids came into town and the weekend was great. We sat down for Thanksgiving dinner. We had a great time. We laughed and reminisced about old memories. When dinner was done, the men got up and went into the family room to watch football and what did the women do? Yep, they got the dishes and walked into the kitchen to clean up.

As I walked by the kitchen, I saw my wife cleaning up and I decided I should stop and see if she needed any help, because she did such a wonderful job putting this weekend together. So I said to her—"Honey you've done a wonderful job with this dinner. Is there anything I can do to help you clean up?" She just about fell over. Then she said, "I'll tell you what. You can take the plates and scrape the food off into the trashcan and then put them into the dishwasher to be washed." I said, "I can handle that." I started scraping off the food into the trashcan and putting the dishes into the dishwasher. About two minutes later, my sons yelled to me from the family room, "Dad, hurry up and get in here, you're going to miss the touchdown." So I started scraping faster and faster, trying to get my job done so I could get in and see the football game. A second time they yelled, "Hurry up, Dad, you're going to miss it." I kept going faster and faster not wanting to leave my job half-done. Finally, I got all the dishes done and then I came to the turkey platter. I just took the platter and I scraped all of the meat off into the trash can.

What do you think my wife said? (I really can't repeat it.) But I said to her, "What's the matter?" She said, "You're wasting food. That could have been sandwiches or soup for the next week." And then I did something that I shouldn't have done. I said, "Well what did it cost? Forty cents a pound?" And I pulled out a $5 bill and I gave it to her! Needless to say, she was not a very happy lady at that point.

Now why do I tell you that story? Was it really the cost of the turkey that upset her? Probably not. What was it then? What probably upset her the most was that I tried to put a price on all the time and effort she'd put into the meal. It really wasn't the cost of the turkey that bothered her. It was all the time and the effort it took her in the preparation to make that dinner. The hours she put into that dinner and the hard work it took to put it together.

Well, you know what happens many times when we leave our kids lump sums of money? Many times they behave like I did, and they take the money and scrape all the taxes right off into the trashcan. (Actually, they send it to Uncle Sam.) They don't appreciate all of the time and effort that Dad or Mom took to accumulate that money. Many times, all they see is the money and do not appreciate the 30-to-40 years that it took to save that money. They don't understand or appreciate that parents often sacrificed and saved in order to set aside some money for the future.

This rising generation is a generation of what? Of spenders. They want it now. My parents grew up during the Great Depression. They lived and served in World War II. Tom Brokaw described this group of Americans as "The Greatest Generation."[13] The Greatest Generation is a generation of savers. They learned what it means to sacrifice today for benefits tomorrow. This generation of savers will be passing their life savings onto the next generation. How they plan and execute that transfer will determine how much the next generation will keep and how much Uncle Sam will get. So unless we take the time and effort to implement exit strategies for our retirement accounts, Uncle Sam will be getting a lot more of our money than he needs to.

I have no desire to leave my kids lump sums of money. None. Because what will more than likely happen if I do? That lump sum will be gone in a very short period of time. But if I can leave them a cash flow on a monthly basis (or an annual basis), then I have been able to accomplish something for both myself, and my heirs.

I know I have spent a lot of time talking about these "tax-infested accounts." But the reason I've spent so much time is because of all of the problems associated with them when the owner of these types of accounts passes away, without any type of distribution plan in place. I reemphasize to you that if we don't have exit strategies for these types of accounts, Uncle Sam loves you! Plan today and take control of your tax planning, to lessen the tax burden your heirs will inherit if you leave them any type of these retirement accounts without an exit strategy in place.

---

13   *The Greatest Generation*, by Tom Brokaw, Random House 2004

CHAPTER 5

STEP #2: INCOME PLANNING

"You've saved $126 for your retirement. My advice is to convert it all to pennies and reinvest it at the nearest wishing well!"

The second step in setting up a safe and secure retirement is establishing a predictable and consistent income stream throughout retirement. We are quickly becoming what I call a "pension-less society." For prior generations of working Americans, it was not uncommon for most people to work their entire career for one company, and then retire with a guaranteed retirement income for the rest of their lives (and many times their spouse's lives as well). That is no longer the case.

As I sit down with people preparing for retirement, I find it is more common for people to have worked for a number of companies, rather than working at only one company for 30 to 40 years.

(Longevity at one company still happens, but it is much less common today than it was in prior generations.) And corporate America has come to realize it no longer wants to take on the risk or burden of those future pension obligations. That is one reason many individual states are experiencing the financial crisis they are today—they are handcuffed to the pension system they have promised to their public employee unions. Corporate America is much quicker and more efficient that governments. Corporate leaders saw what was coming if they didn't change from the older, guaranteed pension-style retirement, where the company was on the hook to pay set retirement benefits, to a system that shifted that risk back to the employee.

That's why companies started shifting from the guaranteed pension plans to the now-popular 401(k) plans. These are plans that don't guarantee a set benefit each year, and shift the risk from the company to the employee and the stock market. So now most employees (not all, but the majority) are *not* guaranteed a retirement income for the rest of their life. They have to do their own income planning based upon how their 401(k) plan has performed over the years. And that can sometimes create problems.

We saw this scenario happen with the financial meltdown in 2008. Many people were getting ready to retire in 2008 and then the stock market crash devastated the value of their 401(k)s. (Many people said they became 201(k)s!) After the crash, they realized they could no longer afford to retire based upon the value of their retirement plan. I had people come in to discuss their situation and they ended up realizing they had to work for another two to five years because of what happened to the value of their 401(k) plan. Had these same people had the old guaranteed pension-type retirement plans with a lifetime income benefit, the stock market crash wouldn't have affected their retirement plan or their guaranteed retirement income.

Who *would* it have affected? It would have impacted the company providing the guaranteed benefits! Their investment portfolio is what would have taken the hit—not the employees' retirement benefits. And this is exactly why corporate America has transitioned away from the defined benefit retirement plans and moved to the 401(k) type plans (defined contribution). It is also the reason why retirement income planning has become so critical.

THE LONGEVITY PROBLEM

One of the new risks of retirement income planning is what we call "longevity risk."

Let me ask you this—are we living longer or shorter these days? Studies show we're living longer than we used to. The average life expectancy for a baby born today is 78 years. And our life-expectancy rate has been climbing higher as our medical technology has gotten better, along with the fact that we're much more health-conscious than we were in years past. In 1970, the average life expectancy was 70 years old. In the 1950s it was 68, and in the 1930s it was only 59.[14]

The longevity risk is a good news/bad news problem. Modern health care has extended our average life span, which is the good news. The bad news is that many of us could ultimately outlive our retirement plan assets if we don't plan properly.

14   National Center for Health Statistics, *National Vital Statistics Reports*, vol. 54, no. 19, June 28, 2006.

Researchers conducted a study of 100 couples who were age 65. They observed the group for 25 years to find out how many of those couples would still be alive at age 90.[15] That is, at least one of the spouses was still alive and would need an income stream to live on. Out of those 100 couples, what percentage do you think either the husband or wife was still alive and still needed income at age 90? The answer is 50 percent! Which means that hypothetically, they needed to plan for an income stream into their 90s.

Half of the couples who are age 65 will still need retirement income in 25 years at age 90.

There was another study done right after the stock market crash in 2008, which asked of a group of seniors the question, "Do you believe you have enough money to last you throughout your retirement?" Some of the answers were predictable, yet some were very sobering. One lady said, "Gosh I hope so. I'm retired and my husband has passed, so there isn't any more money to count on. We both worked hard all of our adult lives and I hope that it will be enough. I am scared though." Another person stated, "Not at the present. We were hit real hard with the market crash. I felt real secure until then. I don't think so now. I don't like thinking about money at this point, it makes my stomach hurt." And finally another responded, "Are you kidding? No. Definitely not. Maybe if I hit the lottery. Money is not a nice subject around our house. I had health problems years ago that caused me to retire in my 50s. Now I wish I hadn't retired."[16]

15   Source: Society of Actuaries RP-2000 table (Healthy Annuitant).
16   Source: Senior Market Advisor, May 2010

Is that the way we want our retirement to be? Worrying if we'll have enough money to last us? As I sit down with people who need to do income planning, I ask them, "How long does this money need to last you?" And you know what their answer almost always is? "The rest of our lives!" I then try to help them realize that the odds that one of them will live into their 90s isn't as remote as it might have been years ago. So setting up a secure retirement income stream is a critical step to a secure retirement plan. They need an income plan that isn't whip-sawed up and down with the economy or with the stock market volatility. I hear it all the time from people who come in and say their broker said, if they plan for a 4 percent to 5 percent withdrawal from their investments for retirement, they should be OK. Well that's fine if everything goes well. Yet do things *always* go well?

An example of the above scenario goes something like this. A couple we'll call Mr. and Mrs. Smith needs $6,000 a month to live on. Let's say they have $1,000,000 in retirement assets in the market. They're getting a combined $2,000 a month from Social Security, which means they need an additional $4,000 a month ($48,000 a year) to meet their monthly income needs. If they earn 5 percent on their $1,000,000 investments, they would have $50,000 a year, or enough to cover the additional $4,000 a month they need. However, what happens when (not if) there's a big stock market correction and their portfolio drops 30 percent, and now their retirement assets are worth $700,000? They still need their $50,000 a year but their portfolio now has to yield over 7 percent to generate the income they need. Not only did their portfolio drop in value, but it also didn't generate the income Mr. and Mrs. Smith needed that year. So they have to go into principal to meet their income needs, which reduces their remaining principal as well. Then they feel like they need to "make up" the money they lost when the market dropped and they take on more risk in order to "recover" their losses—only to lose more principal. It can become a very slippery slope if they don't have a secure income plan that isn't affected by outside influences.

DETERMINING YOUR RETIREMENT NEEDS

As I work with people who are ready to retire and need a retirement income stream, one of the first things I ask them is, "How much do you need each month to live on?" And what I mean by that is— what does it take to maintain their current lifestyle and the way they want to live? And I don't care what that number is. For many older seniors, most of them have their homes paid off. They don't have any debt and so they have a very low monthly overhead that needs to be covered. I've had clients tell me it can be as low $2,000 a month. I've had others tell me they needed $18,000 a month. I really don't care what the number is. I just need a starting point.

WHAT IS A SECURE SOURCE OF INCOME?

The next thing I want to know is what is their monthly income from *secure* sources? Now secure sources mean different things to many people. What do I mean by "secure sources"? When I ask this question at my public workshops, I always get a lot of different answers. I have people tell me rental income, dividends, interest, required distributions, Social Security, pensions, annuity payments. Yet I don't consider many of those answers *secure*.

Is Social Security secure? I'm not sure it's real secure for the long term, based on the current funding model. However, I do feel Social Security will be there for today's planning. I think those people who are currently on Social Security are going to be OK. I don't think the politicians will mess with benefits that are already being paid. I'm not sure what's going to happen in the future, but I do think there will be some changes for the next generation of Social Security recipients (Baby Boomers). Whether it's a reduction of benefits or whether they'll have to wait longer to receive Social Security, something has to change in order to fund those obligations. But for right now, we'll consider Social Security payments a secure source.

> *We are becoming a "pension-less" society in America. We are going to have to be more self-reliant in the future in regards to securing a predictable retirement income stream.*

What else is considered a secure source? Pensions. Annuity payments. What about the other answers? Here's a good litmus test to tell if something is a secure source of income: Can this payment go down? Rental properties can lose tenants. Dividends can drop. Interest rates can come down. So all of these types of investment income can be affected by outside forces. Pensions are usually guaranteed. Uncle Sam sends out Social Security checks each month, as do the insurance companies who are backing annuity payments. That type of monthly retirement income is fairly secure in regards to stability, in that they provide a consistent monthly retirement income stream.

So let's use Mr. and Mrs. Smith again. They need $6,000 a month and they are receiving $2,000 a month from Social Security (Dad's payment is $1,500 and Mom's is $500), with no pension benefit. I like to do what I call an "income fire drill." Do you remember fire drills when you were in elementary school? What happened? The bells would go off and we'd all get up and go out to the playground. Was there ever a fire? No. So why did we do it? We did the drill so we would know what to do *just in case* there was a fire. That's how we should look at our income planning. Do an income "fire drill." Let's look at what would happen if Mr. or Mrs. Smith died and what would happen to their secure income stream.

We should do an "income fire drill" to see what will happen to our income in the event of the death of a spouse.

Now what generally happens to our income on the death of the first spouse? It usually goes down. Why? If Mr. Smith passes away, what happens to Social Security payments? They drop. Example: If Mr. Smith is getting $1,500 a month and Mrs. Smith is getting $500, and Mr. Smith passes away, which one does Mrs. Smith get? She gets whichever one she wants. Obviously she would want her husband's because it's higher, and she does get to choose. But the reason she gets to choose is because what if Mrs. Smith was getting $1,500 and Mr. Smith was the one getting $500? The surviving spouse always gets to pick the highest benefit amount. But Mrs. Smith would lose her own monthly payment of $500, or in other words, she's losing 25 percent of their Social Security income. That's a big hit when we lose 25 percent of our income.

The same thing can be true with pensions and annuity payments, depending on how the survivor benefit is set up. They can have full benefit for beneficiaries, or they can have a partial benefit (50 percent survivor benefit, etc.), or they can go away completely. I had a lady in one of my seminars who came up to me at the break and said, "I want to shoot my husband." I said, "Well, don't do it here, but how come you want to shoot your husband?" Then she said her husband had retired the year before and set up his pension plan so that 100 percent of it goes away when he dies. Now why would he ever do that? The reason is because if you have no survivor benefit, you receive a higher payment now. Was it the correct decision? It all depends. If he lived 30 years, it was probably the right decision because he received a higher benefit for 30 years. If he died in three years, it probably wasn't a good decision. If you can tell me what's going to happen in life, I can probably tell you the right thing to do. The unfortunate thing is we just never know what will happen in the future, and that is why we should have some type of secure income plan in place for the unexpected.

So pensions could go down. Annuity payments could go down (depending on how the beneficiary payouts are structured). All these things come into play as we set up retirement income plans. Again, if we can do an income fire drill and see what will happen when one spouse passes away, then we can properly plan for it.

WHY YOU NEED TO HAVE AN EMERGENCY FUND

Retirement Planning

"It's not hard to set aside 6 month's income for an emergency. There's a guy in Ohio who did it and a woman from Vermont!"

The next part of income planning is setting up an emergency fund. The reason I like to see my clients create emergency funds is because unforeseen expenses always seem to arise (the roof needs repairs, cars need to be replaced, grandchildren have an emergency, etc.). And if we need extra money for some unforeseen reason, we don't want to have to interrupt our investment plan at the wrong time in order to take care of the emergency. You don't want to have to sell stock in a down market because you need funds right away and then take a beating because of bad timing. You don't want to have to do things that will impact your retirement plan negatively.

I generally like to see enough money in the emergency account to take care of four to six months of whatever your monthly needs are. So if it's $6,000, I would like to see $25,000-$30,000 put away somewhere where you can get to it fairly easily if an emergency arises. Psychologically, some people need more than that, and that's OK. Keep enough liquid assets so you feel comfortable. When your roof needs repairs, or your car needs to be replaced, you want enough money available to you to be able to take care of it. You don't want to have to liquidate investment assets in order to take care of these emergencies. You don't want to liquidate stocks in a down market because you need some extra money for the emergency. I really don't care where you keep those funds; however, make sure they are safe and secure and you have access to them.

Proper income planning lets you enjoy retirement without having to worry about whether or not you're going to have enough money to last you for the rest of your life. Income stream is what pays the bills, not assets. If you don't have a proper and secure income stream during retirement, you could end up like one of those people from the beginning of this chapter who don't "like to think about money now. It makes my stomach hurt."

CHAPTER 6

STEP #3:
INVESTMENT PLANNING

"I retire on Friday and haven't saved a dime.
Here's your chance to become a legend!"

L et's move onto the third critical step in setting up a safe and secure retirement plan, and that is our investments. When we talk about investments, we're talking about an exciting and very diverse and opinionated subject. Opinions about investments are all dependent on your point of view. If you ask a real estate broker, they will tell you that real estate is the best investment for everyone. Stockbrokers will tell you that, over time, the stock market is the best. Still others have bought and sold bonds, or commodities, or trust deeds. So it really depends on the background and point of view of each person or advisor as to what is the best investment for retirement.

What are some things that we invest our money in? Real estate, stocks, mutual funds, annuities, bonds, banks, CDs, commodities. There are a lot of things we invest in, and how we invest our money will depend on how old we are and what our risk tolerance is. At the same time, we should understand *why* we invest in the things we do and what we want from those particular investments. Why do we invest in stocks or mutual funds? What do we want our money to do? We usually want it to grow. So we are willing to increase the risk we take in exchange for the opportunity to have our money grow. We are investing for growth. Why do we invest in bonds? What do we get from bonds? We get income from bonds. Some people will tell you that you invest in bonds for safety. Let me ask you this—if interest rates go up, what happens to the value of bonds? They go down. Are interest rates high or low right now? They're probably at an all-time low. So the odds are that interest rates will start going up at some point in the not-so-distant future. And when interest rates go up, what will the value of bonds do? They're going to go down. So I'm not sure it's a good time right now to be going into bonds, but that is an individual decision.

Why do we put our money in banks or CDs? Because it's safe or secure (certainly with interest rates so low, we're not putting our money there for income). And we invest in municipal bonds or annuities because of their tax benefits.

LET YOUR GOALS DETERMINE YOUR INVESTMENTS

When investing for retirement, the question to ask is, what do we want our retirement to be like? What are some the hopes, and dreams, and goals most of us have when we retire? If I told you that you had enough money to last you the rest of your life, how would that make you feel? Wouldn't it make you feel secure? Isn't that one thing that all of us want to feel in retirement? We want security.

What else do we want in retirement? Most of us probably want the freedom to do what we want. Maybe we want to travel all over the world or go to Hawaii for three months. We want to have options to do what we want. We can give our children (or grandchildren) annual gifts of $13,000—*if* we want to. So we want the freedom and option of doing what we want. And most of us want what I call peace of mind and quality of life in our retirement.

Investment Planning

1	2	3
Investments	Objectives	Retirement Goals
Stocks	Growth	Feel Secure
Mutual Funds	Income	Good Health
Real Estate	Safety	Freedom
Bonds	Tax Benefits	Options (travel, etc.)
CD's		Peace of Mind
Annuites		Quality of Life
Commodities		
Businesses		

Let me ask you this question—which of these three columns is most important to you in retirement? Which of these columns is what you want your retirement to be like? When I ask people in my workshops to answer this question, most of the time they usually all say it's the last column. Aren't these the things we really want in retirement? These are the kind of things that we hope our retirement will be like. So Column 3 is actually the most important. However, it's pretty hard to get the things in Column 3 without getting the things in Column 2, isn't it? So wouldn't you agree that the things in Column 2 might be the second-most important? And probably the least important of these is Column 1.

Investment Planning

Tools

3	2	1
Investments	Objectives	Retirement Goals
Stocks	Growth	Feel Secure
Mutual Funds	Income	Good Health
Real Estate	Safety	Freedom
Bonds	Tax Benefits	Options (travel, etc.)
CD's		Peace of Mind
Annuites		Quality of Life
Commodities		
Businesses		

You know who taught me this concept? It's been the people I've met with over the 30 years I've been in this business. What I have found out, as I've helped people plan their retirement, is that people want to feel secure. They want the freedom and options to do what they want. They want peace of mind and they want the quality of life that comes with good health. So in reality, Column 3 really is the most important to us and Column 1 is least important. What this tells me is that the things mentioned in Column 1 are really just the *tools* we use to achieve the hopes and dreams in Column 3.

DON'T BECOME "MARRIED" TO YOUR INVESTMENT TOOLS

But you know what else I've learned over the years? Many times people become "married" to their tools—their investments! Now why do I say that? Let me explain what I mean by becoming married to our investment tools.

In the late 1990s, the stock market got carried away in the dot-com mania and eventually reached an all-time high (up to that point) in January 2000, when the Dow Jones hit right around 11,700. Then the dot-com bubble burst and the market dropped to down around 7,400 in 2002. We lost approximately 38 percent in a little over two years. Then things turned around and we had a nice bull market and it climbed back up over the next five years and in October 2007, it hit an all-time high at 14,164. Then we had the financial meltdown in 2008 and the market crashed all the way down to right around 6,600, a loss of approximately 53 percent in a year and a half. And now it has climbed back up to where we are today, at around 11,000 - 12,000 (plus or minus, depending on the day).

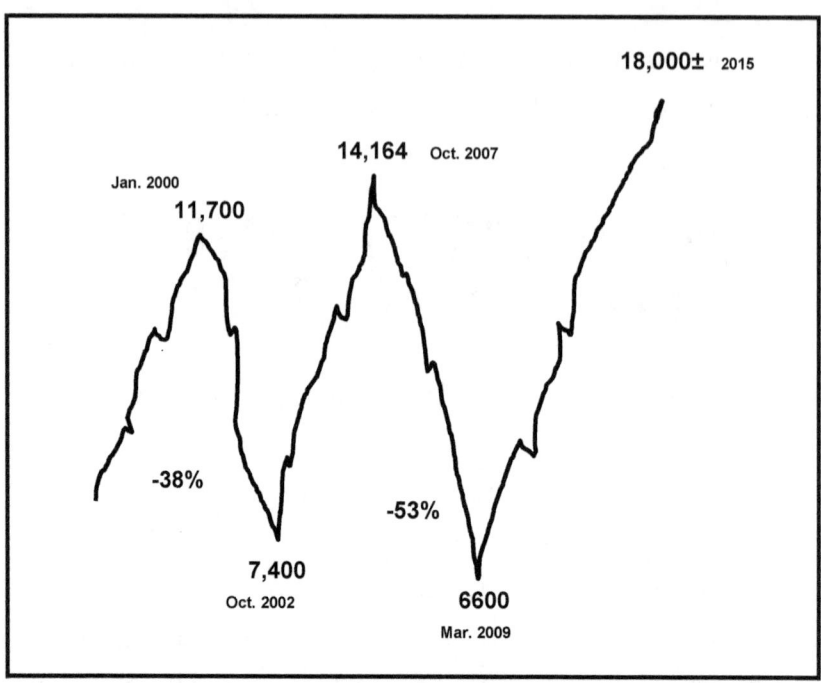

In the market, we want to buy when and sell when? We want to buy low and sell high. So that means that all of us bought when the market was at 7400 and sold when it was at 14,000—right? No? (When I ask the people at my seminar this question, everyone laughs and they usually say they buy high and sell low.) Why don't we do that? Why don't we buy low and sell high? There are two or three reasons why we don't do it that way. You know why we don't sell? One reason is that we develop an emotional attachment to some of our investments (again, becoming married to our investment tools). Maybe we have some stocks or mutual funds that have done well for us during our working years and we just can't seem to emotionally let go of them, even though we have transitioned into retirement. We tell ourselves that it will come back and it will be a good investment again. We become "married to the tool" we've used for so many years. Yet now that we're retired, we should actually position our investments to protect the principal rather than try to "hit the home run."

GREED KILLS

Another reason we don't sell is that we get greedy. When the market was having its bull run in the mid-2000s, we thought the market was going to go where—18,000? So we don't sell even though we've made a lot of money over the past few years. We want more. We get greedy!

When I was working with people back in the early 2000s, when the market was crashing and it had dropped down from 11,700 to around 10,000, I mentioned to many of them that they may want to consider getting out of the market, and they'd say "I can't get out now, Dan. I want to wait until it gets back up to 11,000. Once it gets back to 11,000, then I'll get out." Isn't that what you hear all the time? When the market drops, many people say they'll get out when the market gets back to where it was.

The stock market is driven by two things—emotion and instant information, neither of which anyone has control of.

So when the market turned around in 2003 and started climbing back up, once it got to 11,000 (where people said they wanted it to be, so they could sell and get out), did these same people then sell and get out? Probably not. Why? Because the market was going up and they were seeing the big returns on their statements again. They got greedy and they had a very short memory of the sick feeling they had when the market crashed and they lost all that money. People did make some nice gains in the next few years; however, they also lost most of those gains in 2008 when the market crashed and dropped 53 percent from its all-time high. And what do these same people tell me today? They say they'll get out when the market gets back to 14,000. So they become married to their tools.

I find it interesting that the things people want most out of retirement—to feel secure and enjoy their retirement years, is many times at the mercy of the investment tools they use. If feeling secure is the most important thing to them, then what happened when the market crashed in 2008? Did they feel secure? If not, then why not change the "tools" they're using to let them feel secure? But rather than changing the tools they use, they keep them and hope that the market comes back. Many times feeling secure takes a back seat to the tools, rather than changing the tool so they could feel more secure in retirement.

NOBODY KNOWS WHAT THE MARKET WILL DO

Stockbrokers are just as guilty when it comes to becoming married to investment tools. What did your broker tell you in 2008 when the market crashed? "Don't feel bad, everyone else in the market lost money as well! Just hang in there, it will come back! We're in this for the long-haul." That's easy for them to say—it's not their money! What else can they say? "Sorry I screwed up your retirement!" If they said that, you'd be long gone. So they tell you to just hang in there and everything will be OK. They tell you not to panic and sell because you then "lock in your losses." (Again, rather than changing the investment tool and feeling secure—they tell you to keep the tool and forfeit the security.) The question you then want to ask them is, "How long do I have to wait?" It's one thing to ride out the market cycles when you're young and working and you have time on your side; however, the older we get, the less time we have to recover. Do you think stockbrokers know if the market is going to go up or down? Absolutely not. If they did, they would have gotten all of us out when the Dow Jones was at 14,000. But they don't know where the market is going any more that the rest of us do, because the market is driven by emotion, and no one knows from one day to the next what is really going to happen. So my philosophy has always been, "It's not how much you make, it's how much you keep!"

DON'T BE AFRAID TO PAY TAXES ON YOUR GAINS

The final reason we don't sell at the top of the market is because we don't want to pay the taxes on the gains. Many times as I sit with people and discuss the investment part of their retirement plan, if they have a lot of money in the stock market and they have a lot of capital gains, I might suggest moving some of that money into a more conservative position. On more than one occasion, they don't want to do that—or won't do that—because they would have to pay taxes on the capital gains, and they don't like paying taxes. They just have an aversion to paying taxes. So I ask them this question—what is the capital gains tax today—15 percent? Is that a high or low tax bracket? They tell me it's a low bracket. In fact, it's one of the lowest brackets we have ever had. (The only lower bracket is 10 percent for those earning $0 - $8,500.) So if they sold their stocks (or mutual funds) when the Dow Jones was at 14,000, they would have had to pay taxes on 15 percent of the capital gains and be through with it. But because of their aversion to paying taxes, they rode the market crash all the way down and ended up losing 50 percent on those same investments. Does that make sense? When we have capital gains, that means we did something right! It means our investments actually gained money! So paying capital gains could actually be a good thing—and we're paying those taxes at a very low rate. Yet many times we're so resistant to selling a stock or mutual fund that has gone up in value, either because we're greedy or because we don't want to pay the taxes, that we'd rather risk losing those gains when the market has a correction. What happens is that the stock or mutual funds ends up losing more money than the 15 percent we would have paid in capital gains taxes.

As we move into retirement, we really need to step back and make sure we're not "married" to our investments. We should be willing to make the necessary changes in the investment tools we use in order to eliminate the risk to our retirement assets. We should realize that when we move into retirement, it is a fundamental change in our lifestyle. We move from earning money to living off our assets. Doesn't it also make sense that if we have a fundamental change in our lifestyle, we should make a fundamental change in how we invest our money?

STEP #3:
INVESTMENTS (CONTINUED)

Investment Phases

"That's it. Have a good cry. Get it out and then we can decide where we want to invest what's left of your money!"

We go through three phases in our lives in regards to our investments. The first phase is what I call the *accumulation* phase. This is the time when we are working and accumulating our assets in preparation for retirement—in other words, this phase is our working years. It is the phase when we can take a little more risk with our assets because we are younger and we have the time to ride out big swings in the market, and we also have time on our side to make up the losses. (Yes, there will be losses.) We are hopefully accumulating enough assets to take us through our retirement years and provide the lifestyle we want in retirement.

The second phase we go through—or at least we *should* go through—is what I'll call the *protection* phase. This phase comes as we move close to retirement (or we're already in retirement). In this phase our approach changes from accumulating assets to protecting those assets. It's the time when we should move away from a more aggressive investment philosophy to a more conservative approach. It's the time when we should concentrate on protecting what we have.

The third phase is what I call the *distribution* phase. This is the time when we implement our retirement and income plan. This is the time we should set up a solid foundation for the future income we need or desire in retirement. How we set up the distribution phase of our assets will have a big impact on how much we get to keep and how much of our money we're going to give to Uncle Sam.

IT'S NOT WHAT YOU MAKE BUT WHAT YOU KEEP

I would like to spend some extra time talking about the second phase mentioned above – protecting our assets. Sometimes it's very boring protecting our money. There's no "excitement" to safe and secure returns. Yet in retirement, it's not about what you make, it's about how much you keep and about protecting yourself from loss. The example below illustrates this point.

If you take a $100,000 investment and have two different investment accounts—one which has the potential for higher returns yet also the risk of losing principal versus a much lower but guaranteed return. Which account provides a better return after three years if one of the riskier accounts has a bad year? Obviously this is just an example, yet it helps drive home the point of keeping what you earn. Many times the "safe investments" are very boring and not very exciting; yet again, it's not how much we make—it's how much we keep!

$100,000 Investment			
7% Return	$107,000	3% Return	$103,000
7% Return	$114,490	3% Return	$106,090
-7% Return	**$106,475**	3% Return	**$109,273**

There was a study done a few years ago where researchers examined the deaths of those who died climbing Mount Everest, to find out how and where most of the deaths occurred. After collecting the data on 212 deaths from 1921-2006, do you know what the results of the study showed? It showed that the majority of climbers who died climbing Mt. Everest actually died *on the way down*, after reaching the summit. The majority of climbers had reached the summit of the tallest mountain on earth, only to die on the descent.[17]

Why do I tell you this story? Well, I have seen and worked with many people over the past 30 years who have worked all of their

17   *British Medical Journal,* December 20, 2008

lives—30 or 40 years "climbing the financial mountain" in life, so to speak. Many have saved and sacrificed during that time, hoping to have enough money to retire on. They reach their goal and make it to the top of the financial mountain and then are prepared to sail off into the retirement sunset, only to "die" on the way down (retirement) because they don't protect the assets they have. They either become married to their investment tools, they get greedy, or they don't do proper planning for their retirement. Whatever the case may be, their retirement plan is not what they had hoped it would be.

Let me give you an example of this. Suppose you have a $100,000 investment in the stock market (individual stocks and/or mutual funds) and the market has another crash and it drops 50 percent in value. Your $100,000 investment is now worth $50,000. But the very next year it rebounds and the market goes up 50 percent. What happens to your investment? Let's take a look:

EXAMPLE:

Investment in stock market	$100,000
-50% drop in market	-$50,000
Account Value:	$50,000
+50% Market Increase	$25,000
	(50% of the $50,000 account balance)
Account Value:	**$75,000**

So you can see, even though the market went down 50 percent and then back up 50 percent, your gains were only half of what you lost, because you were earning the gain on only half of the account value you started with. The market would have to increase 100 percent for you to get back to where you started.

I have had people come in for consultations and when we talk about their investments, they say with pride that they earned 20 percent on their investments the previous year. Then I ask them where they are in comparison to where they were before 2008. And almost every time they say they've made some of their losses back, but they still are not back to where they were before the crash. Again, it's not how much we make, it's how much we *keep*!

///

"Rule #1 for investing: Never lose money! Rule #2: Never forget Rule #1."
—WARREN BUFFETT

///

The unfortunate thing about this example is that it is exactly what happened to many people in 2008 when they were getting ready to retire—only on a much larger and more important scale. Many people had accumulated their 401(k) plans (or other retirement assets) and they were ready to retire when the stock market crashed, and their retirement accounts crashed with it. After the crash, they couldn't afford to retire because their assets wouldn't generate the income they needed. Yet had they moved their assets into the "protection phase" the closer they got to retirement, the market crash wouldn't have affected them and they still could have retired when they had planned.

THE PROBLEM WITH "TARGET DATE FUNDS"

Many times I have people ask me how they can protect their 401(k) plan when the plans are usually limited to mutual funds. Some retirement plans have tried to address this issue by offering what is called "Target Date Funds," which are supposed to be managed by professional fund managers. Fund managers are *supposed* to begin moving your 401(k) investments into more conservative mutual funds, the closer you get to retirement. In a target date fund, you tell the fund manager the year you want to retire, and as you draw closer to that retirement date, they move your money to more conservative investments (or are at least that's what they're supposed to). Unfortunately, it doesn't always work that way. The following quote is from an article about target date funds in *The New York Times* in 2009.[18]

Washington blessed them as a way to put your 401(k) on automatic pilot and glide safely toward retirement. But popular target-date mutual funds have badly missed the mark — and now regulators are asking why.

The Securities and Exchange Commission and the Labor Department are examining why the funds, which were supposed to become safer as their investors grew older, seemed to get riskier instead.

Big mutual fund companies like Fidelity and Vanguard promised that target-date funds would shift automatically

---

18   *The New York Times*, "Target-Date Mutual Funds May Miss Their Mark," Leslie Wayne, June 24, 2009

from high-growth investments, like go-go tech stocks, toward safer ones, like bonds, as investors neared the year of retirement — a "target date," like 2010, 2020 or 2030.

....But as the stock market plummeted last year, some 2010 funds — which many investors thought would be invested safely by then to protect their nest eggs — lost 40 percent of their value. That showing was even worse than that of the Standard & Poor's 500, which fell 38.5 percent....

So even many of the target funds, which were supposed to protect employees' 401(k) assets the closer they got to retirement, ended up losing as much (or more) than the market did in 2008.

IN-SERVICE TRANSFERS: TAKE CONTROL OF YOUR 401(K)

If you would like to get control of your 401(k) assets and have the opportunity to invest those assets the way you want, there is a little-known law in the tax code that allows individuals to take advantage of what is known as an "in-service transfer." This provision allows employees who are age 59½ (or older), still employed, and participating in their company's 401(k) plan (or other types of retirement accounts, i.e., 403b, 457, etc.) to exercise a direct transfer of the funds from their company's plan to an IRA they can control—without any taxes.

You can still participate in the 401(k) plan as you always have; however, you now have the assets in your own IRA, which were in your 401(k), and you can now invest them as you see fit.

Keep in mind that the provisions vary from company to company regarding in-service transfers. Some plans only allow contributions the employee has made, along with any gains on those contributions, to qualify for the in-service provision. Other plans allow full transfer of funds. Some companies may have a vesting schedule for company contributions, others don't. But this provision is something that isn't well known among employees.

In-Service transfer rules allow owners of retirement accounts like 401(k)s to gain control of their funds before they retire without any tax consequences.

So if you are 59½ and still employed, you may be able to gain control of your retirement assets by utilizing the in-service transfer provision allowed by the IRS. Companies don't have to provide this provision in their plan documents; however, the in-service transfer option is becoming almost the standard and most large 401(k) plans allow it. The unfortunate thing is that companies don't always tell their employees about in-service transfer rules because it reduces the overall plan assets, which might affect the cost of administering the plan. Make sure you ask about it. Over the years, I have helped many clients take control of their retirement assets *before* they retire using the in-service transfer option provided in their plan documents. It is one simple way you can reduce the risk to your retirement assets.

RISK ISN'T WORTH IT

The next thing to think about when you're in the protection phase is risk. When I sit down with people to do retirement planning, I want to get to know them and what their goals for retirement are, so I always try to ask them how long it took them to accumulate their money. The answer is almost universally the same: it took them all their lives to accumulate what they have. Then I follow up with another question. How much of this money can they afford to lose? And because they've either just retired or are planning to retire soon, they almost always answer that they can't afford to lose any of it. Yet when I look at where they have their investments, many times they've got a majority of them sitting in a volatile stock market (either in mutual funds, stocks, or a managed brokerage account), with no downside protection to those assets. And many times when the market has a drop in value, they become nervous and "freeze" because they're not sure what to do and they end up not doing anything. Instead, they sit and watch the value of their investments fall with the rest of the market.

Most of the time, the investment return on retirement assets will probably not change your lifestyle all that much— so why put that money at risk?

For those of you who are already retired, think of your situation for a minute and then think about this question. Whether you earn 5 percent on your money, or you earn 12 percent on your money, is it really going to change your lifestyle in retirement? As I work with people and analyze their situation, we discover that their lifestyle really won't change, regardless of the return they get on their investments. They have sufficient assets to provide the retirement income they need. Their monthly income needs are fairly manageable. So whether they earn 4 percent to 5 percent on their money, or 10 percent to 12 percent, it really won't change anything about their lives. The only real impact it could have is a little more money for their heirs. So my question to them is, "Why do you risk putting your retirement in jeopardy by keeping it in an emotional and volatile stock market where a severe market correction could affect your entire retirement?"

It's not how much money we make that counts—it's how much money we keep!

I'm not saying the stock market is bad. There is a time and a place for taking advantage of the potential returns the stock market has to offer. There have been many, many, many people who have made their fortunes in the stock market. But the time to utilize the market is when you are younger and have time on your side to make up any losses you will experience. (Not "might" experience—we all will experience losses in the market.)

BE A SINGLES HITTER, NOT A HOME RUN SLUGGER

I always stress the concept that when we retire, we should be moving from the accumulation stage to the protection phase with our investments. Sometimes I describe the protection phase in baseball terms. For example, would a baseball player's batting average be better if he hit a home run every second time at bat and struck out the other, or if he simply hit a single every time he came to the plate and never struck out? I'd take the second batting average every time. Reggie Jackson is in the National Baseball Hall of Fame as one of the greatest home run hitters in the history of baseball. Do you know who holds the major league record for strikeouts? Reggie Jackson.[19] Reggie hit a lot of home runs, but he also holds the record for strikeouts. That's what sometimes happens when you're trying to hit one out of the park. In retirement, we don't have to hit home runs. We just need to hit a lot of singles (getting a safe and secure return) and minimize striking out (losing money). If we just take care of our money we're probably are going to be OK. It's when we try to swing for the fences and get greedy that the market ends up coming back to bite us. Slow and steady growth without losses is the key. We should concentrate on hitting lots of singles rather than swinging for the fences, trying to hit a home run.

Despite everything we've just talked about, stockbrokers are convinced that the stock market is the best tool for everyone—no matter what their situation. They rationalize this belief by selling "conservative" stocks or mutual funds, or using bonds for older clients. However, are so-called "conservative" stocks or mutual funds

---

19   Major League Baseball Stats: http://MLB.com

still really where retirees ought to be? If the market goes down 40 percent and the "conservative" stocks or mutual funds only go down 25 percent, is that still OK in retirement? I met with people during the market crash of 2008 and many of them stated that they didn't realize how risky their stock portfolio was until it was too late. And the reason their brokers never told them about the risk was because the market was in a bull market and the returns made the broker look good. The catch is that you can't get those big returns without exposing your principal to higher risk. We sometimes just trust our stockbroker when he tells us something is a good stock or mutual fund and many times we don't know what we really have or what risk we're exposed to until it's too late. And sometimes we really don't know anything about what we've bought, other than that our broker said it was a good stock.

Avoiding losses in a down market is what secures and protects a portfolio in retirement.

It's like the story about the stockbroker who was an unscrupulous guy, willing to sell anything to anybody—whether or not they were a prospect or client, or whether or not it really was the kind of investment he told them it was. He was just happy to make the sale. When this stockbroker dies, he goes to heaven and meets St. Peter at the Pearly Gates. St. Peter says to the man, "We have a new program. You get to decide whether or not you want to go to heaven or hell." The stockbroker thought that was a pretty good deal, knowing that he really didn't treat his clients they way he probably should have. The stockbroker says to St. Peter, "Great. Let's go down to hell and see what hell looks like." They get in the elevator and they go down to hell. They open the door and they walk out on a nice white sandy beach. Palm trees blowing in the wind, surfers in the water. The stockbroker tells St. Peter, "Hey, hell doesn't look too bad. Let's go up and see what heaven looks like." They get in the elevator and they go up to heaven. They open the door and it's kind of boring, just people sitting around on clouds, playing their harps. Not a whole lot going on in heaven. The stockbroker says to St. Peter, "I think I'm going to choose hell. It seems like it's a lot better back down in hell." They get back in the elevator, they go back to hell, they open the door, and they take the stockbroker and they throw him into a pit of fire and brimstone. Startled that he didn't get what he thought he was getting, the stockbroker said to the devil, "This isn't what I saw when I first got here." The devil responded, "That's what we show to prospects, now you're a client!"

Many times people don't understand how exposed their investments really are to risk until it's too late.

We need to know what we're getting and why we buy the investments we do. Many times we're like the stockbroker choosing between heaven and hell and we're not getting what we think we're getting. The biggest challenge I have in working with people and planning their retirement is getting them to move from the accumulation phase to the protection phase. They have been in the accumulation mode for so many years and they're so worried about having enough money to last their lifetime, that they are hesitant to take some of their assets out of the market to establish the safe and secure foundation they really need for their retirement. This concept of establishing a safe and secure foundation for your retirement will determine whether or not you will be one of those in retirement who can really S.W.A.N. ("sleep well at night").

CHAPTER 8

STEP #4: NURSING HOME EXPENSES AND THE COST OF LONG-TERM CARE

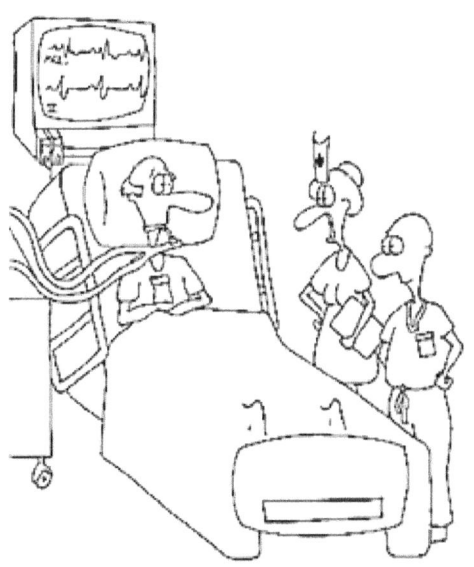

"Your insurance won't cover your ventilator any longer, so Bob here will be giving you mouth to mouth for the next several days!"

The fourth step in protecting our retirement in this financial storm is planning for the possibility of nursing home expenses. Most of us don't want to even think about going into a nursing home. It's a subject that isn't very pleasant, so many times we just don't think about it. But if we don't plan for this possibility, it could potentially devastate our entire retirement plan. So we should at least figure out what we might do and how we could address the cost of a nursing home, in the event we do end up in one.

The cost of 24-hour nursing care can easily run over $75,000 per year.

A report published by *The Wall Street Journal* stated that for a couple who are both age 65, the chances that at least one of them will need long-term care in a nursing home will be at least 50 percent.[20] The average length of stay for someone in a nursing-care facility is just under 2½ years (combined for men and women).[21] Now those figures take into account the people who break their hip and are just trying to recover, as well as those admitted for longer terms with diseases such as Alzheimer's, Parkinson's or whatever else might require long-term care assistance. But the average stay is 2½ years.

According to "The Guide to Nursing Homes" website, the average cost of a nursing-care facility varies from state to state. Where I live, in California, the *average* cost for a semi-private room

---

20　*The Wall Street Journal* , January 22, 2008
21　Statistics on Nursing Homes and Their Residents, California Medicare Coalition, 2008

is $214 per day, and a private room is $284 per day. That's more than $77,000 a year! Can your cash flow and retirement plan afford that expense—in addition to the living expenses for the spouse not in a nursing facility? If you can't, then how do you go about paying for that?

I generally hear three different responses from people when it comes to dealing with the possible issue of nursing-home costs. The first person says they're not going to worry about it because it won't happen to them. Yet statistics tell us that 50 percent of us, age 65 or older, will spend *some time* in a nursing home. Again, the average stay is 2½ years. The person who says they're not going to worry about it because it won't happen to them really isn't dealing with the facts. They're like the guy who went to the doctor and said, "Doc, my wife is losing her hearing, she doesn't answer my questions or listen to me anymore." The doctor tells him, "Let's do a little test and find out how bad her hearing really is. When you go home, get about 20 feet behind her and ask her a question. If she doesn't answer you, walk up about ten feet, ask her the same question. If she still doesn't answer you, keep moving up closer to a point where she turns around and answers you. Then we'll know how bad her hearing is."

Later that night, the man is in the family room watching TV and his wife is about 20 feet away in the kitchen fixing dinner. The husband says to his wife, "Honey, what are we having for dinner?" No answer. So he gets up from the sofa and walks to within 10 feet of his wife and asks her again, "Honey, what are we having for dinner?" Again, no answer. He moves up right behind her and says a third time, "Honey, what are we having for dinner?" His wife turns around and she says, "I've told you three times we're having chicken!" It's not always the *other* person that it happens to! Sometimes it's us. Fifty percent of us are going to spend some time there. It may not ever happen, but what if it does?

The second person says they're not going to worry about long-term care expenses because if they need long-term care they're going to move in with their kids and let their kids take care of them. Boy, that's just what your kids want to do! But in reality, because they don't plan for this kind of risk, many people do end up having to move in with their children. Often they don't have the funds to provide long-term care or they have too many assets, which disqualifies them for government assistance so they don't have anywhere else to go. There are solutions to this problem that we will discuss later in this chapter.

50 percent of people age 65 or older will spend some time in a nursing facility.

The third type of person acknowledges the possibility of needing long-term care and understands the costs involved, so they want to plan for the unexpected. That's the most sensible approach.

So what are some of the things we can do to plan for the unexpected costs of nursing home expenses? What is available to us to address this issue?

HOW LONG-TERM CARE INSURANCE WORKS

The answer is that there are a variety of things we can do to plan for the costs of nursing care. When I talk about long-term care in my seminars, I ask about paying for nursing home expenses, and people respond that they could buy long-term care insurance. That is definitely an option available to us. Then why don't we all go out and buy long-term care insurance? The answer is because it costs so much. That's true, long-term care insurance does seem to cost a lot. But what determines the cost? Well, our age at the time we take the policy out; whether we have health issues; how long we want the benefits to be paid (two years? four years? 10 years? a lifetime?) and the daily benefit desired. These are all things that factor into the equation when determining the cost of long-term care insurance.

Then I have people who say they don't want to buy long-term care insurance because they might not ever go into a long-term care facility. They say they might die from a heart attack and then they would have paid all those premiums for nothing. I don't buy into that reasoning for a couple of reasons. Let me explain why with the following example.

Do you or any of your friends own a house that is free and clear with no mortgage on it? For this example, let's assume you own a single family home, and you own the home without a mortgage. Would you carry fire insurance on it? You probably would. Why? Does anyone require you have fire insurance? Nope. No one. For those of us who have not paid off our mortgage yet, our mortgage company requires us to keep homeowner's insurance on our home. But once we pay off our home, no one requires us to carry fire or homeowner's insurance. So why would you buy fire insurance? We do it to protect ourselves *just in case* there is a fire.

Now here's the question for you. Do you hope your house burns down so you can use your fire insurance? Probably not. We actually hope we never have to use our fire insurance. But we buy and carry that insurance to protect ourselves just in case something does happen. Yet I talk to people all the time and they say, "I don't want to buy long-term care insurance because I might pay for 10 or 15 years and spend money on all those premiums and then have a heart attack and die and never get to use the insurance." You know what I say to that? Sign me up! If I never have to spend a day in a nursing home, sign me up! We're willing to pay for fire insurance (or car or medical insurance), and if we don't have a fire or car accident, do they give us our premiums back? Absolutely not. So why should we expect to get money back from long-term care insurance if we don't ever go into a nursing home?

The reason we might want to consider long-term care insurance: just in case.

The reason most of us get different types of insurance is to shift the risk of various things to the insurance companies. We don't want to take the chance of getting hurt and needing hospital care and then having to pay an exorbitant medical bill—so we buy medical insurance. We don't want to take the chance of getting in a car accident and then having to assume the cost to repair our car—so we purchase car insurance. Or, we don't want to have to replace our home at our own expense in case our home burns down—so we buy fire insurance. We're willing to shift the risk of those costs to an insurance company—in exchange for paying premiums.

We carry insurance just in case we do have a house fire or car accident. So just like other types of insurance we purchase, we can shift the cost of long-term care to insurance companies in exchange for premiums.

The average stay in a nursing facility is 2½ years.

So what does long-term care insurance cost? Obviously, it depends on our age, our health, the benefit amount we want, and how long we want the benefit to last. But let's assume it costs $5,000 a year for a benefit of $6,000 a month ($72,000 a year) and we end up paying that premium for 10 years and then we have a heart attack and die. We've spent $50,000 and never got to use the insurance. We'd be out the $50,000. But what if rather than having a heart attack, we have a stroke instead, which is more likely, and now we need to be in a nursing home? How much does the policy pay us the very first year? $72,000! And the second year? $72,000. And if we're there for a third year, how much would it pay? $72,000. So we've paid out $50,000 in premiums and we ended up getting back $72,000 the very first year, and a total of $288,000 over four years. The reason long-term care insurance costs so much is because 50 percent of us are going to need it sometime. The insurance companies know this. And the cost of care once you go to a nursing home is so expensive the insurance companies need to charge enough to cover it.

HOW TO REDUCE THE COST OF LONG-TERM CARE INSURANCE

However, there are ways we can reduce the cost of long-term care insurance. My philosophy has always been that we should plan for long-term care expenses to provide a safety net against possible long-term costs. Just like other types of insurance, we can usually afford the deductibles in order to get our car or home repaired. In the same regard, we can probably afford a three-to-six-month stay in a nursing facility. What has a tremendous impact on our assets and retirement plan is an extended stay at $6,000 a month. So maybe rather than having a 90-day deductible, we could increase the deductible to 180 days (meaning the insurance company doesn't pay any benefit for the first six months). I can handle $36,000 out of pocket, but if I'm in a facility for three to four years, then the insurance company is going to be paying most of that cost. By increasing the time before the insurance company is responsible, it has the same effect as increasing the deductible on our car insurance—it reduces the premium. It might reduce it by 30 percent or more (depending on the daily benefit you want).

Another option to reduce the cost of long-term care insurance is to limit the number of months the insurance company will pay the monthly benefit. As stated earlier in this chapter, studies have shown that the average length of stay in a nursing facility is just under 2½ years. So maybe rather than having a lifetime benefit, you could limit the benefit to four to six years. When we limit the benefit payout period, the insurance companies know what their exposure is and they can reduce the premium accordingly. But when we have a lifetime benefit, that creates an unknown exposure to the insurance company so they have to price a policy accordingly.

As I have worked with people in retirement planning, cost has always been one of the roadblocks to purchasing long-term care insurance. Yet when I show my clients a few different options where they can reduce that cost, many times they implement this safety net to protect against the possibility of extended costs for long-term care.

Most people I talk to about planning for long-term care expenses usually feel like they'll deal with it with their own assets. And that's perfectly OK if there are sufficient assets and they have the cash flow to fund the cost of long-term care. Normally I wouldn't recommend this approach unless your assets are at least several million dollars and we know there are sufficient assets to last long enough for retirement. However, when clients have several million dollars, I find that they understand the concept of transferring the risk to insurance companies for possible future exposure. So even though their cash flow can cover the cost of long-term care, they usually shift that risk and purchase long-term care insurance—just in case!

HOW ASSET PROTECTION PLANNING WORKS

A final option for addressing nursing home expenses is by doing what we call "asset protection" planning. When done properly, this option can allow clients to qualify for government paid long-term care, while at the same time protecting their assets from the required spend down in order to qualify for assistance. If some type of asset protection planning isn't done, then in order to qualify for government-paid long-term care (Medicaid), individuals are required to "spend-down" their assets until their assets are under the allowed limit.

In order to be eligible for Medicaid benefits, a nursing home resident may have no more than $2,000 in "countable" assets. The spouse of a nursing home resident—who is called the "community spouse"—is limited to one half of the couple's joint assets up to $109,560 in "countable" assets (this figure changes each year to reflect inflation).[22] In addition, the "community spouse" may keep the first $21,912, even if that is more than half of the couple's assets. This figure is higher in some states, even up to the maximum of $109,560.

Long-term care insurance may or may not be the best answer for everyone. However, "asset protection planning" should be part of every retirement plan.

Quoting from the guidelines of Medicaid: All assets are counted against these limits unless the assets fall within the short list of "non-countable" assets. These include the following[23]:

- Personal possessions, such as clothing, furniture, and jewelry.
- One motor vehicle is excluded, regardless of value, as long as it is used for transportation of the applicant or a household member. The value of an additional automobile may be excluded if needed for health or self-support reasons. (Check your state's rules.)

22 Department of Human Services: DC Medicaid and Spend-Down Eligibility
23 Department of Human Services: DC Medicaid and Spend-Down Eligibility

- The applicant's principal residence, provided it is in the same state in which the individual is applying for coverage (the states vary in whether the Medicaid applicant must prove a reasonable likelihood of being able to return home). Under the Deficit Reduction Act of 2005 (DRA), principal residences may be deemed non-countable only to the extent their equity is less than $500,000, with the states having the option of raising this limit to $750,000. In all states and under the DRA, the house may be kept with no equity limit if the Medicaid applicant's spouse or another dependent relative lives there.
- Prepaid funeral plans and a small amount of life insurance.
- Assets that are considered "inaccessible" for one reason or another.

So in essence, if a couple has one of the partners enter a nursing home, they have four options when it comes to covering the cost of the long-term care:

1. They have purchased long-term care insurance and the insurance company will cover the cost of that care—after the initial deductible is satisfied.

2. They can move in with their children and let their children shoulder the burden of the long-term care of the parent.

3. They can self-insure and pay for the cost of the care from estate assets (assuming the size of the estate is adequate).

4. They can qualify for government assistance that requires either the spend-down of estate assets to the required level (which is not a very exciting option to me), or they can implement an asset protection plan in advance that keeps

the majority of assets in place, while allowing the person needing the care to qualify for Medicaid assistance without having to liquidate their assets for the cost of care.

Asset protection planning can be implemented in a variety of ways, ranging from setting up a gifting program to children to reduce estate assets, to utilizing what is called an "Irrevocable Defective Grantor Trust." But the reason you have to do this type of planning in advance is because when trying to qualify for government assistance for long-term care, the government does a "look-back" for the past five years to see if you've given away assets in order to qualify. So any monetary gifts given away within the past five years are included in determining the value of estate assets. Asset protection planning takes into account what the costs for long-term care will be for the first five years and then sets enough assets aside to cover the cost of care for five years. The remaining estate assets can be gifted away once a person enters a nursing home because we have already set aside enough assets to cover the cost for five years, and we can gift to any children the remaining assets, which won't be counted against them at the end of the five years.

Although no one really likes to talk or think about the possibility of going into a nursing home, the likelihood of needing long-term care is increasing every year. With 50 percent of the people who are age 65 or older needing some type of long-term care sometime in their life, and with the average stay in a nursing facility at approximately 2½ years, the cost of long-term care is one of the greatest threats to a viable retirement plan. Each generation is living longer, and that in turn creates an increased chance of needing long-term care at some point. The planning for nursing home expenses should not be overlooked. And the reason to do asset protection planning is to make sure one's assets aren't wiped out through the required government spend down, in the event of having to enter a nursing home.

Obviously each situation is handled differently depending on the size of the estate and the overall estate distribution plan for the eventual heirs. But don't be one of the people who say they'll worry about it if or when it happens! Too many people have taken that approach, only to have their entire assets wiped out when they *could* have planned ahead—but didn't.

CHAPTER 9

STEP #5: ESTATE PLANNING & LEGAL DOCUMENTS

"I'm sorry Mrs. Wilkins, but your husband's will specifically stated that he wanted to be buried next to you!"

The fifth and final step you can take to help your retirement plan withstand the perfect financial storm is to make sure your legal documents are up to date and in place when needed. Even if you have implemented everything we've talked about in this book up to this point, if you don't implement the final step of setting up proper and effective legal documents, then all of the planning you *have* done could go to waste. So this final step is one of the most critical in your retirement plan.

In 2001, President Bush signed the Economic Growth and Tax Relief Reconciliation Act, which gradually increased the federal estate tax exemption over the following 10 years, and reduced the maximum estate tax on inherited estates. The estate tax exemption in 2001 was $675,000 and the new law increased that exemption over the next 10 years until the estate exemption was actually unlimited in 2010. However, the downside of this legislation was that the estate tax reductions were not permanent. The tax cuts were temporary and they ran out at the end of 2010, which was when the debate in Congress took place. Unfortunately Congress didn't help us much when the federal inheritance-tax debate was taking place in 2010. All Congress did was "kick the can down the road" for two years. So they did what they have been doing in the recent past and only temporarily addressed the issue. The Democrats wanted to lower the inheritance exemption in order to increase tax revenues, while the Republicans wanted to eliminate the estate tax, claiming it represents double taxation. What they ended up doing was compromising for two years and just put a Band-Aid on the problem. The resulting compromise in Congress was a two-year law passed in December 2010—the Tax Hike Prevention Act. That compromise set the estate exemption at $5 million, but only for two years. Then Congress was finally able to work together and get a bill passed in 2012 (American Taxpayer Relief Act) which set the estate exemption permanently at $5 million dollars (indexed to inflation). However, as history has taught us, one thing for sure is that we can expect our tax laws to change in the future. But for now, we finally have estate tax rates that for the time being—are permanent.

Finally—a permanent estate tax law we can count on for planning purposes!

HOW REVOCABLE LIVING TRUSTS WORK

So what has been the most common legal document used over the past 25 years in estate planning and legal documents? It is probably a *revocable living trust*. These trusts have been used extensively over the past few decades to help individuals and families transfer assets from one generation to the next.

Revocable living trusts have become popular for several reasons. However, when I ask people why this estate document has become so popular, the number one answer people give is that this document helps heirs avoid probate. Avoiding probate has become the main reason people use a living trust for their main estate document. Heirs or beneficiaries who have had to deal with the probate system will tell you it is a very frustrating, time consuming, and expensive way to pass assets onto heirs. And so avoiding probate is an excellent reason to use a trust. If properly drafted, a revocable living trust avoids the probate system and allows assets from an estate to be passed onto the heirs without government involvement. I have had personal experience with the probate process (which I will share with you at the end of this chapter). Trust me, you usually want to do everything you can to prevent the courts from administering the distribution of your estate—because you lose control of the assets.

It is estimated that over the next decade, this generation will be part of the greatest transfer of wealth from one generation to the next in our nation's history.

Are there other reasons (other than avoiding probate) that trusts have become so popular? Absolutely. There are a number of additional reasons; however, let's focus on the reasons that are most important to you.

How about controlling assets after you've passed away? Through a revocable living trust, you can dictate how your assets can be passed to children or other beneficiaries. Earlier in the book we talked about parents having one (or more) children who can't manage money. (I think I called them "idiots.") So parents can utilize the trust to structure how they want their estate distributed if some of their children can't handle money effectively, if parents don't trust their son or daughter-in-law, if grandchildren are too young to inherit lump sums of money, or if they just don't want to leave lump sums of money to their heirs. Control is also a viable benefit for using a revocable living trust.

Another benefit from utilizing a trust is that the estate remains private. No one knows the estate assets other than those who are beneficiaries, along with the trustee(s) of the trust. A properly funded trust stays out of the probate process and as such, it does not become part of the public record. Do we know how much the assets are in the Kennedy estate? No—because the assets are transferred through trusts and they stay out of the probate process. A trust can keep your estate private and out of the public eye.

And finally, depending on the size of the estate, a trust can possibly save estate taxes for the heirs. Utilizing an A/B Revocable Trust has the ability to double the estate tax exemption for the heirs.

Let's assume your estate is worth $7 million dollars (I know, some of you have more, some of you have less, but for this example, let's use the $7 million figure). The current estate exemption is $5 million (indexed to inflation from 2012). If an estate is passed on through a will, what happens is on the death of the first spouse? All the assets are passed onto the surviving spouse. Then when the surviving spouse passes away, the entire $7 million estate will be passed onto the heirs in one lump sum. For easy calculation, let's assume the current estate exemption is $5 million, leaving $2 million subject to estate taxes of 40%[24]. This approach would end up creating a $800,000 estate tax bill for the heirs of the estate.

If the same estate were passed on with an A/B living trust, on the death of the first spouse, half of the estate ($3.5 million) would be placed in the "descendent trust" (let's say it's Trust A) and the other half is place into the "survivor trust" (Trust B). The surviving spouse has access to the assets in both trusts if necessary. Yet when the surviving spouse passes away, there is only $3.5 million in each trust, thus falling under the estate exemption of $5 million and avoiding any estate tax (saving the $800,000 in taxes if the estate were passed on though a will). That being the case, using an A/B Trust will basically double the estate exemption which would allow a $10 million estate to be passed onto heirs without any estate tax (under current law).

---

24 American Taxpayer Relief Act 2012

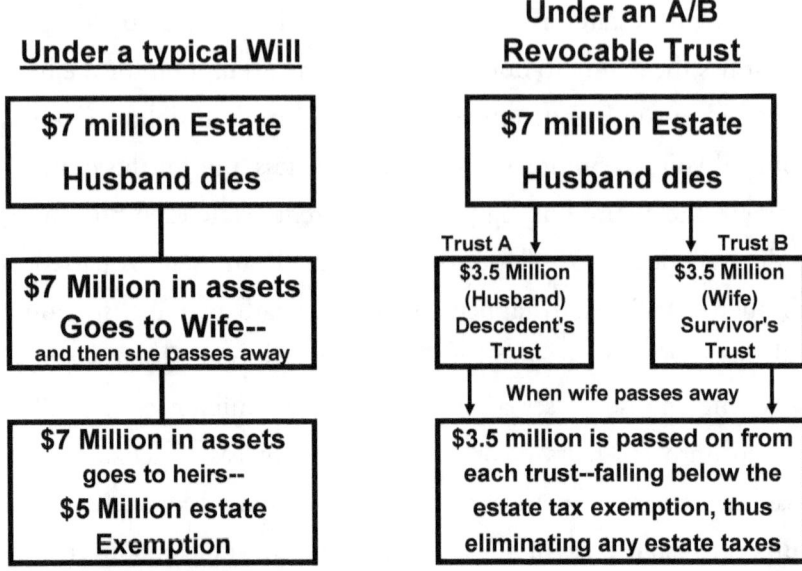

Under a typical Will

| $7 million Estate |
| Husband dies |

↓

| $7 Million in assets |
| Goes to Wife-- |
| and then she passes away |

↓

| $7 Million in assets |
| goes to heirs-- |
| $5 Million estate |
| Exemption |

$2 million taxed @ minimum 40%
$800,000 estate tax

Under an A/B Revocable Trust

| $7 million Estate |
| Husband dies |

Trust A ↓   Trust B ↓

| $3.5 Million (Husband) Descedent's Trust | $3.5 Million (Wife) Survivor's Trust |

When wife passes away ↓

| $3.5 million is passed on from each trust--falling below the estate tax exemption, thus eliminating any estate taxes |

WHY YOU NEED DURABLE POWERS OF ATTORNEY

Other estate planning documents you should have are durable powers of attorney. We want these in place, again, "just in case." We hope we never have to exercise our power of attorney because that would mean we're incapacitated in some way. But we want them in place—just in case something does happen—an accident, a stroke, mental incapacity, or anything that would cause us not to be able to effectively manage our estate.

So, what kind of powers of attorney should we have? We should have a power of attorney for health care in order to have someone available to make health care decisions for us—if necessary. We should also have one to cover our financial affairs, as well as one for medical records. If we don't have a power of attorney for medical records, then if we have a stroke and our children want to move us to another state to be closer to them, and they ask our doctor for a copy of our medical records, the doctor can't release those records (because of privacy restrictions) unless there is a power of attorney authorizing the release of that information.

Obviously the larger the estate, the more advanced the planning needs to be. The use of life insurance trusts, special needs trusts (for disabled heirs), along with charitable trusts are all available for those estates which require advanced estate plans. The key is to make sure you have a current plan in place along with updated documents.

WHAT PRINCESS DI AND JIMI HENDRIX CAN TEACH YOU ABOUT YOUR ESTATE PLANS

Over the years, I have found there are numerous mistakes people make when it comes to this step in their retirement plan. The following is a list of some of the most common mistakes along with examples of famous people that committed (or omitted) them.

1. **Doing Nothing:** If you don't plan your own estate while you're alive, you could end up like Jimi Hendrix and have someone you barely knew controlling your estate. Hendrix's estate was fought over in court more than 30 years after he died.

2. **Doing It Yourself:** Former Supreme Court Justice Warren Burger created his own will with 176 words, but he left out key provisions and his family paid the price.

3. **Not Updating:** Heath Ledger never updated his will after the birth of his daughter, leading to chaos and family members fighting through the press.

4. **Taking Shortcuts:** Princess Diana used a "letter of wishes" leaving personal items to her godchildren, instead of specifying her wishes in a will or trust.

5. **Not Letting Your Loved Ones Know Where Your Estate Documents Are Kept:** Olympian Florence Griffith-Joiner's original will couldn't be located and her probate estate took over four years to close.

6. **Failing to Finish What You Start:** Michael Jackson created a trust, but he never fully funded it, defeating the primary purpose of having a trust in the first place. And we've all seen that this led to public family fights in probate court.

7. **Making Verbal Promises:** Marlon Brando's housekeeper said Brando made oral promises to her of a home and continued employment, which led to two separate lawsuits after his death.

8. **Procrastinating:** Sonny Bono passed away at the age of 62 without a will in place. This lead to many complications, including a secret love child who surfaced and wanted part of Bono's estate.

9. **Leaving Your Intent Unclear:** Whitney Houston's father, John, named Whitney as a beneficiary on a large life insurance policy, but it was unclear if he wanted Whitney to keep the money or to turn over the money to her step-

mother. This confusion led to a two-year court battle, which is still ongoing.

10. **Choosing an Untrustworthy Executor or Trustee:** Doris Duke chose an unsavory trustee—her butler—to manager her $1 billion foundation. When he used assets for himself, it led to an expensive fight in court that cost the charities Duke wanted to benefit.

I would like to close this chapter with a personal experience I had with the probate process and share with you the story of a couple who were clients of mine. It will help to illustrate what can happen when your legal documents are not up to date.

This couple was older, and had been married for more than 50 years. They became clients of mine later in their lives and I suggested they look at updating their legal documents. Their trust had been drafted many years prior to our relationship, estate tax laws had changed over the years, and their choice for a successor trustee had already passed away. They didn't have any children and their desires for their estate distribution had changed. The husband was legally blind (he was born blind) and he had met his wife when she was working at a blind center he attended. Obviously, the husband was very dependent on his wife for all of their financial decisions, as well as the other aspects of their lives.

Unfortunately, they procrastinated and never got their documents updated, and then the wife unexpectedly passed away. In order for the husband to maintain his independence, he hired a caregiver to come in and live with him. (You've heard of these stories before, right?) This situation was exactly what we've all read about when dishonest caregivers attempt to take advantage of those they're supposed to take care of.

The caregiver had only been employed for a little over a month or so, and she had convinced the blind husband to add her as one of his estate beneficiaries. I was somewhat skeptical and we still needed to get his trust document and other estate documents updated, especially now that his wife had passed away. So I arranged for him to meet with an estate planning attorney to update his estate planning documents. This is where the story gets interesting.

Within two weeks from meeting with the attorney, and before the attorney could complete the documents, the husband also passed away, leaving the estate in limbo. The caregiver then produced two *hand-written* notes—written by the caregiver and supposedly signed by the husband, leaving over $50,000 to the caregiver. Luckily for the heirs, I had a relationship with the couple prior to the caregiver, but unfortunately, the estate documents were not current. The successor trustees listed in the trust documents had all passed away prior to the couples' deaths. So in order to keep the caregiver from getting the $50,000 she wanted, I had the attorney put the estate into probate to preserve the assets for the heirs. Another unfortunate thing—there were 32 beneficiaries listed in their outdated trust document, made up of nieces and nephews spread out all across the country. It was a mess.

To make a long, expensive and time-consuming story short, because the couple didn't have any children or close relatives, we were able to get the courts to agree to allow me to act as the successor trustee for the trust. Had I known what lay ahead, I probably would have declined. Personal property had to be disposed of. Real estate and cars had to be sold, some of which had to be discounted in order to get cash to distribute to the beneficiaries, all of which took time and effort. Although this process did take an extraordinary amount of time, I was able to prevent the caregiver from getting the $50,000 she was seeking. The court invalidated the handwritten notes, but the unfortunate part of this was although the probate process did prevent the caregiver from getting the money she was trying to get, it took over 2½ years and more than $50,000 in legal fees and court costs before I was able to close out the estate and have the courts sign off on the estate distribution to the 32 beneficiaries. It is a prime example of how the best-laid plans for estate distribution can be torpedoed when estate documents are set up incorrectly or are not up to date.

We might have a great idea of how we want our retirement plan to work and how to best pass our assets onto our heirs; however, if we don't take the final step in our retirement planning and set up proper estate documents, then our entire planning process can go out the window, especially if we don't use the tools available to us, or we allow those tools and documents to become outdated.

CONCLUSION

I've discussed a lot of different things in this book. I'm sure there are many other advisors, stockbrokers and "investment professionals" who might emphasize other important steps they feel are necessary to include for a secure retirement plan.

I have found, with more than 30 years of experience, that the five steps discussed in this book are the *foundation* to a safe and secure retirement. Yes, there will be debates about different investment philosophies, like what amount of risk is appropriate for retirees, or the advantage or disadvantage of a traditional IRA versus a Roth IRA. There will be opinions on just about everything from tax planning and qualified plan distribution to estate planning. You will have opinions on whether or not to plan for asset protection against nursing-home expenses or to purchase long-term care insurance. There will always be differing opinions on any topic we discuss. Yet what *isn't* debated is that people who are retired (or preparing to retire) want to feel comfortable and confident that they have a safe and secure retirement plan in place; one which will not be negatively impacted and torpedoed by the financial storms around them.

Advisors, stockbrokers and financial planners are a dime a dozen. You can find one on just about every corner who will be happy to invest your money for you. What you need to do is find someone who has the same philosophy as you, and who will help you set up the plan based on what *your* hopes and dreams are, not based on what they want to sell you. A plan that allows you the freedom to enjoy life in your "golden years" without having to worry about those unforeseen economic disasters that appear to be all around us. A plan which gives you the ability to have the kind of retirement you envisioned as you worked toward this time of your life.

The important thing to remember is to make sure the foundation of your retirement plan is secure. Make sure there's a safe stream of income coming in, so no matter what financial storm hits, your retirement and lifestyle aren't impacted by an unexpected financial tsunami. It's a lot like a house—we want a strong foundation that will survive when the storms hit. If we don't have a strong foundation, then our house crumbles under the storm. There's nothing wrong with trying to take a little additional risk in order to make a little higher return—with a portion of our assets. But we don't want to take that risk until we have the foundation of our plan secure.

I hope this book has helped you in evaluating what you need to do to protect your retirement in the future against the financial storms that are here (and the financial storms that are sure to come). Make sure you are working with someone who understands what your goals are and who will help you establish a safe and secure retirement plan. I hope your retirement is all you dream it will be and you are one of those lucky ones who can S.W.A.N. (sleep well at night!).